Their Duty Done

OUT FOR VICTORY.

TOMMY.
"I want Peace right enough—but I'll finish my job first."

The Kitchener Battalions
of the Royal Berkshire Regiment

1918

Colin Fox
John Chapman   Martin McIntyre
Ian Cull   Len Webb

Foreword by Peter Simkins

Cover Photograph
The cadre of the 5th Battalion under Lieutenant-Colonel H T Goodland being welcomed at Reading GWR station on 18 June 1919 by their first Commanding Officer, Colonel F W Foley.

Photographs which accompany the text are taken from family papers, authors' collections and *Berkshire and the War* (by kind permission of the Reading Evening Post). Individual acknowledgement is given of those photographs reproduced by kind permission of the Trustees of the Imperial War Museum.

Designed and typeset by Julie Colman and Laura Gingell, students at the Department of Typography & Graphic Communication, The University of Reading.

Printed in the Department of Typography & Graphic Communication, The University of Reading.

Further copies can be obtained from:
The Centre for Continuing Education
(Extramural Studies)
The University of Reading
London Road
Reading
RG1 5AQ

© The contributors 1998

ISBN 0 704911 62 0

Contents

Foreword iv
Acknowledgements vii

1. Introduction   1
2. The German Spring Offensives 1918   3
3. The 8th Battalion during the German Offensive   7
4. The 5th Battalion during the German Offensive   16
5. Final Allied Offensive   24
6. The Battle of Amiens   28
7. The advance to Péronne   33
8. Attacks at St Pierre Vaast Wood   42
9. Towards the Hindenburg Line   46
10. The last weeks: 5th Battalion   54
11. The last weeks: 8th Battalion   57
12. Disbandment   63

Appendices

I. Short biographies of local men who served with the battalions in 1918   67
II. The Hudson family, a tribute from Wing Commander T H F Hudson (rtd)   76
III. Prisoners of war   78
IV. Visiting the battlefields today   86
V. Casualties and commemorations   89
VI. Casualty statistics 1915–1918   104
VII. Honours and awards   108

Sources   114

Foreword

For the officers and men of the British Expeditionary Force on the Western Front, 1918 was a year of near disaster and eventual triumph. Its start was not propitious, for in January the British Fifth Army had to take over an additional stretch of front from the French as far south as Barisis – some five miles beyond the Oise. To compound its difficulties, the defences bequeathed to the Fifth Army by the French were rudimentary. In February and March, manpower problems caused a reduction in strength of the British infantry divisions under Haig from twelve battalions to nine. Then, between 21 March and 6 June, divisions of the BEF found themselves directly in the path of three of the major offensives – in Picardy, in Flanders and on the Aisne – which were launched by Ludendorff in a desperate bid to win a decisive victory in the West before the presence of the Americans tipped the scales irrevocably against Germany. These offensives, at least in their initial stages, came dangerously close to success, plunging the BEF deep into its worst crisis since the autumn of 1914. In contrast, and having survived the worst that the Imperial German Army could throw at them, Haig's British and Dominion divisions represented the tactical and technological cutting edge of the Allied armies in their final 'Hundred Days' offensive of August to November 1918 – winning, in the process, what John Terraine has called 'the greatest succession of victories in the British Army's whole history.'

The 12th and 18th (Eastern) Divisions, which contained, respectively, the 5th and 8th Battalions of the Royal Berkshire Regiment, were centrally involved in these dramatic events, as this book admirably describes. Both divisions made an important contribution to the blunting of Ludendorff's March offensive, though in different settings and circumstances. The 12th Division in Byng's Third Army, helped to bring the German advance to a halt near Aveluy, close to the division's fields of endeavour and sacrifice in 1916. The 18th Division fought as part of III Corps in the Fifth Army in the southernmost sector near the Oise between 21 and 26 March, before moving to the Villers-Bretonneux sector, where it played a key role in the defence of Amiens between 31 March and 27 April. Indeed, by my calculations, elements of the 18th Division were in action for a longer period in the March - April fighting, and took part in more attacks and counter attacks at Villers-Bretonneux, than any other British or Australian division.

The tactical conditions confronting the BEF in 1918 were quite different, for much of the year, from those which prevailed during the comparatively static warfare of 1915 to 1917. In March command and control from the higher headquarters often broke down or were rendered ineffective by the depth and initial pace of the German advance. Relatively small groups of officers and men were frequently called upon to stand firm for an hour or two, holding a wood, ridge line or crossroads to cover the withdrawal of their comrades before falling back to a similiar position a mile or so to the rear where they might have to do the same thing all over again. Costly and exhausting as this process was, such small-unit operations undoubtedly helped to slow down and blunt the German thrust. In addition, the experience made those that survived more accustomed to decentralised command and rapid decision -making at a lower level. This, in turn , stood the BEF in good stead -especially its divisional, brigade and battalion officers - when it was obliged to adapt once again to the semi-open warfare of August–November 1918.

In the Hundred Days, the two divisions – by now largely composed of conscripts aged eighteen and a half and nineteen and a half – served together in III Corps, of Rawlinson's Fourth Army, in August and September and both remained in action virtually to the end – the 12th Division until 29 October and the 18th until the 5 November. During these weeks, the 12th Division had five prolonged spells in the line or in actual battle, suffering 6,904 casualties in some of the heaviest fighting of the offensive. Not for the first time, the 18th Division too saw more action than most, despite the fact that, at times in mid-September, the average strength of its companies was no more than seventy men. The prolonged nature of their ordeal notwithstanding, the 12th and 18th Divisions achieved respective success rates of 69.5 percent and 78 percent in opposed attacks during the Hundred Days.

Apart from shared battle honours, the two formations had other things in common in 1918 – not least the high quality of their commanding officers. The 18th Division was commanded by Major General Richard Lee, a Sapper of 'quick grip and decision' according to the divisional historian, Captain G H F Nichols – Lee being seen at his best in the mixture of big set-piece assaults, frequent forward movement and small unit manoeuvre which characterised the Hundred Days. The 12th Division was led, from April onwards, by Major General H W Higginson, who had been an outstanding brigade commander in the 18th Division in 1916 and 1917 and was arguably one of the most gifted – and underrated – tacticians in the BEF. The 6th and 8th Royal Berkshires had both served under Higginson in 53rd Brigade before he was elevated to the command of the 12th Division.

Above all, the two divisions and their Berkshire battalions stand as splendid examples of what ultimately could be achieved by the citizen soldiers of Kitchener's New Armies, even after the chaotic and unpromising early days in 1914. This excellent publication – for which Colin Fox and his colleagues deserve considerable praise – should stand as a fitting tribute to the officers and men of two battalions which, by 1918, demonstrated how far the BEF had improved since the Somme and whose collective courage and powers of endurance contributed as substantially as any other formations to the defeat of the Imperial German Army.

Peter Simkins
Senior Historian
Imperial War Museum

Acknowledgements

We should like to acknowledge the support we have been given in the research, the writing and the production of this booklet.

For giving us access to private papers and guiding us to useful sources we thank:
Mr Alan Ault
Mr Tim Lamb
Mr Stephen Reinstadtler
Mr Andrew Tatham
Mr Paul Taylor

For his contribution on a distinguished family whose members have played a part in all the volumes in our series we are most grateful to Wing Commander T F H Hudson (rtd).

During the whole period of our research we have received helpful guidance from the staffs of the following institutions:
Berkshire County Reference Library, Reading
Commonwealth War Graves Commission, Maidenhead
Imperial War Museum, London
Newbury Public Library
Public Record Office, Kew
Royal Gloucestershire, Berkshire and Wiltshire Regiment (Salisbury) Museum and its curator, Major J H Peters MBE, who has been a good friend of the project for the last five years.

We are grateful to another firm friend, Mr Peter Simkins, Senior Historian at the Imperial War Museum. He gave us encouragement from the start and we were delighted that he was able to accept our invitation to write the Foreword for this final volume.

To Dr Julia Boorman of the University of Reading we once more offer warm thanks for giving time to read drafts of the material and offering constructive comments. Any errors or omissions in the final version are of course our responsibility.

To Julie Colman and Laura Gingell and the Department of Typography and Graphic Communication of the University of Reading we are indebted for the design, typesetting and printing of the booklet.

1 Introduction

This volume, the fourth in a series on the Kitchener battalions of the Royal Berkshire Regiment which served on the Western Front, brings their story to a conclusion.

For one of the battalions, the 6th, the war came to a premature end. In late January 1918, whilst the men were still in the Ypres Salient where they had spent the last months of 1917, they received the news that their battalion was to be disbanded and the troops dispersed to other units. The destinations for most of the men were to be other battalions of the Royal Berkshire Regiment; almost half would be going to the 2nd Battalion and many of the remainder to the 1st. Farewells were said by the Battalion Commander on 29 January and by the 53rd Brigade Commander on 30 January. Disbandment began a week later and was completed on 22 February.

Private A J Gosling, who had been with the battalion since his enlistment at Abingdon in December 1914, expressed his feelings in a post-war memoir:

> 'In February (sic) we were informed that the whole British Army was to be reorganised and that our battalion was to be split up. This came as a bitter blow to those of us who had been with the battalion since its foundation.'

The disbandment of the 6th Battalion was part of the general reorganisation of the British Expeditionary Force early in 1918 which followed from a government re-ordering of priorities based on the assumption that the war was likely to last until 1919, if not 1920. As far as allocation of manpower was concerned, the army now had to come after the navy, and also after ship building, aircraft and tank production. In January 1918 Field-Marshal Sir Douglas Haig as Commander-in-Chief was instructed to reduce his British divisions from twelve to nine battalions and to disband two of his five cavalry divisions. The 6th Royal Berkshires were one of the 141 New Army and second-line territorial battalions which then ceased to exist.

The fortunes of the two remaining Royal Berkshire Kitchener battalions in 1918 were of course determined by the role played by the infantry divisions of which they formed a part. Throughout the war the 5th Battalion served with the 12th (Eastern) Division. The 8th Battalion, having in 1915 been assigned to the 1st Division, remained with them until the February 1918 reorganisation, when it took the 6th Battalion's place in the 18th (Eastern) Division. Here it experienced the full force of the German offensive as it opened on 21 March and remained heavily engaged until a week before the armistice was declared in November.

During the retreat of March and April 1918 the two battalions were in different sectors, the 5th to the north of the River Somme, the 8th to the south. In the following chapters which cover this period, their actions are dealt with separately. When the Allied counter offensive was launched in August, 12th and 18th Divisions were neighbours in III Corps, fighting alongside each other until the end of September. The narrative here brings the battalion strands together. For the final weeks of the war, 12th Division was moved further north and the two stories separate once more.

As far as the men are concerned, we are dealing in this volume with battalions quite different from those formed in response to Kitchener's call. Many of the volunteers of 1914 and 1915 did not survive the Battle of Loos or the Somme campaign. From 1916 they were being replaced by conscripts, with a higher proportion of younger men. From the beginning the Royal Berkshire battalions never were 'Pals' battalions in the sense of those recruited for example in the large northern cities with a shared local or employment background. The proportion of Berkshire men in the original three battalions was not much more than one third. By 1918 this proportion had been further reduced and local connections were therefore further attenuated.

What the men had in common was what lay before them, the ordeal of battle. There are no simple answers to the questions of what motivated the original volunteers to join up or what enabled the conscripts to face up to their ordeal. Our account of the two battalions' experiences in the last year of the war closes with a quotation from Captain G H F Nichols, historian of the 18th Division. He enumerates some of the characteristics and qualities of what he calls a 'plain English Division' and in doing so echoes the present volume's title. The notion of doing one's duty may seem prosaic or today somewhat out of fashion, but in its implicit unselfishness and modest idealism it is to be respected.

This series is dedicated to the memory of those who did their duty.

2 The German Spring Offensives 1918

The German High Command decision to mount a series of major offensives in the west starting early in 1918 was made against the background of events which had taken place in the previous year: the entry of America into the war in April 1917 and the exit of Russia (confirmed by the peace negotiations which had opened in Brest Litovsk in December). The weakened state of Germany's allies, Austria – Hungary, Turkey and Bulgaria, together with evidence of crumbling morale on the home front were further spurs to action. In combination, these strategic factors made imperative an attempt to use the temporary superiority in numbers achieved on the Western Front by the transfer of German divisions from the east. This superiority was enhanced by the straitened circumstances in which the British Expeditionary Force found itself in early 1918, recently reorganised, under-strength in front-line infantry and with five divisions helping out on the Italian front.

German planning was directed by General Ludendorff, First Quartermaster-General, together with the Chiefs of Staff of two of his Army Groups. In the first offensive, code-named 'Michael', with its northern extension 'Mars', the initial objective was to break the British front between the Rivers Scarpe and Oise, using an advance in the south to secure the German flank and then wheeling north-west to force the British back towards the Channel. The first main thrust would fall at the juncture of the British and French armies, on the southern part of the British front held by the Fifth Army under General Gough.

By March 1918 Ludendorff had 192 divisions available in the west, 74 of them facing the 26 of the British Fifth and Third Armies combined. An imbalance of strength between the two British armies gave General Gough's Fifth Army 12 divisions to hold a 42-mile front whilst General Byng's Third Army had 14 for 28 miles. Not only were the British divisions under-strength; their new defensive positions, particularly in the south, were both incomplete and manned in such a way as to leave too many troops in the exposed forward zone and not enough in the battle zone where the main fighting was in theory to take place. Construction of defences in a third, a rear zone, had hardly begun.

The German tactics were designed to take full advantage of these weaknesses. Their assault would be based on surprise, using only a five-hour preliminary bombardment which would be followed by infantry attacking in loose formation and led by specially trained 'storm troops'. These units would aim at deep penetration of the British positions, bypassing strong points, over-running artillery positions and rupturing lines of communication. This tactical surprise would be aided on the day by the use of gas and, as it turned out, by thick mist shrouding the battlefield.

The German bombardment opened at 4.40am on 21 March. A total of almost 6,500 guns had been assembled which, following the British practice at the Battle of Cambrai, were able to fire without pre-registration. In addition to paralysing the British defence, the artillery provided a barrage behind which the German troops began their advance five hours later. In sharp contrast to the British at Cambrai, the Germans would be relying entirely on their artillery and infantry. They had no tank force of any size; indeed of the nine tanks deployed on 21 March five were captured British Mark IVs. Spurning the use of cavalry, the Germans would have no means of exploiting a breakthrough should it come.

At 9.40am the German infantry moved swiftly through the forward zone on the Fifth Army front and took it within an hour and a half. A penetration of some four-and-a-half miles was achieved on the day, less against some of the stronger defences of Third Army to the north. British losses were high, disproportionately but understandably (given the German 'infiltration' tactics) in prisoners, – some 21,000 out of 38,500 total casualties.

By the end of the second day of the battle the Fifth Army had been isolated on both its flanks and had committed all its reserves. Third Army also had to give ground, retiring over the old Somme battlefields but holding its positions around Arras. The speed and momentum of the German advance could not however be sustained, and when by early April the British defences in front of Amiens still held firm, the first phase of the offensives was over, with a 40-mile advance but without a strategic advantage having been won.

The second phase – 'Georgette' – followed on 9 April, by which time changes in the Allied command structure had given General Foch the responsibility for coordinating the action of the French and British armies. Gough had been penalised with removal for the performance of his Fifth Army, his place taken by General Rawlinson with a re-designated Fourth Army.

'Georgette' initially took the form of an attack on a 12-mile front between Armentières and Béthune south of the River Lys, followed the next day by a thrust north of the river on a shorter front against the Ypres salient. Such rapid progress was made by 11 April that Haig on that day issued his celebrated 'Backs to the wall' appeal. The Channel ports would be threatened if Ypres and Hazebrouck (only 22 miles from Dunkirk) fell; neither did, although the Salient was reduced to its small-

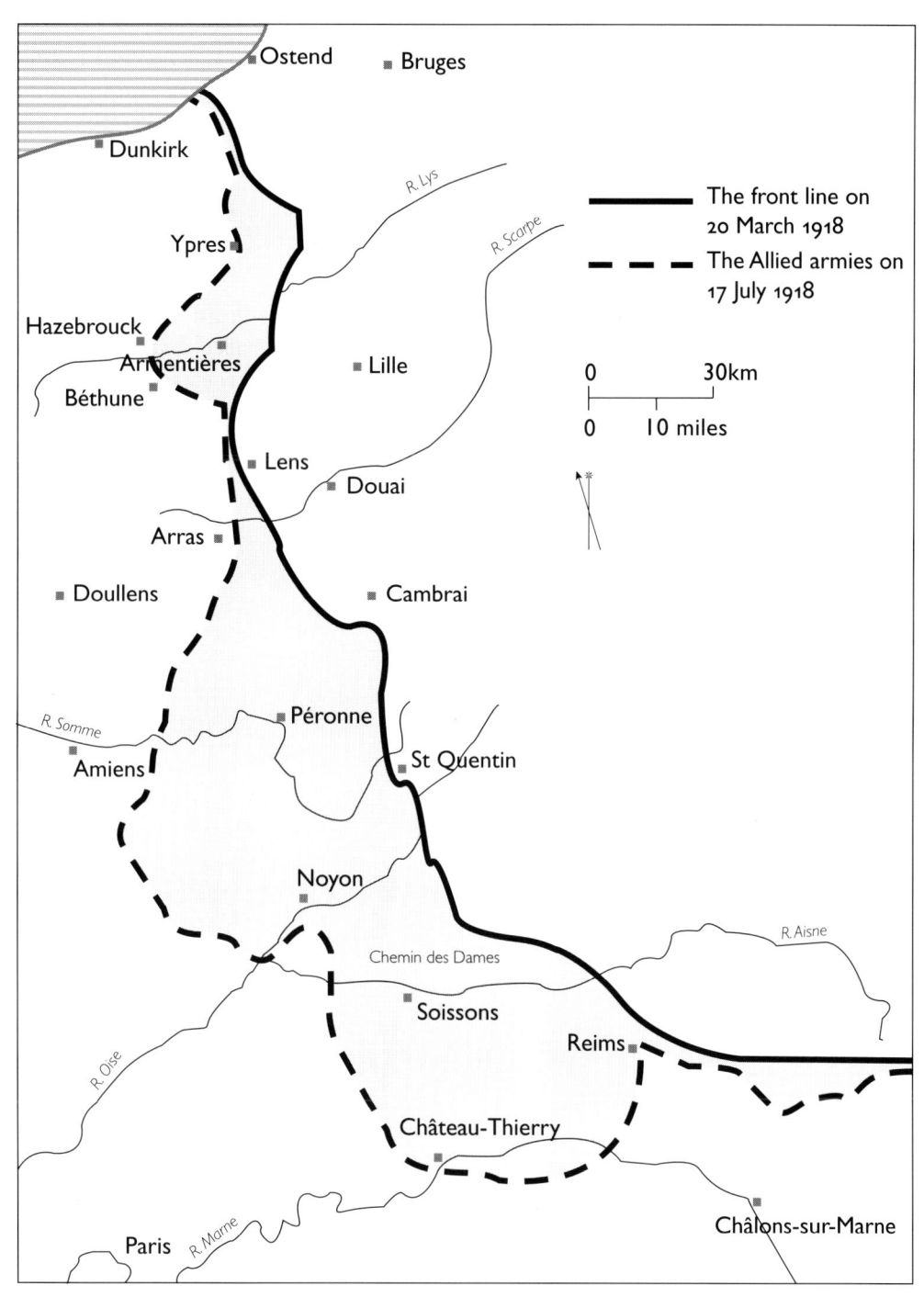

German territorial gains in the 1918 offensives

The German Spring Offensives 1918

est size with the loss of both Messines Ridge and Mount Kemmel and with German troops at Hellfire Corner. A last bid to break through to the Channel failed on 29 April. Here, as further to the south, German territorial gains brought with them no strategic advantages – and American troops were by now arriving in Europe at the rate of 15,000 a month.

Battle of Hazebrouck. Walking wounded coming back. Near Merris, 12 April 1918 (IWM Q10293)

American units, seven complete divisions in France by 1 May, were to play a part in stemming one of the last main thrusts of the German offensives against the mainly French-held front on the River Aisne. Four British divisions sent there on rest were to suffer heavily on the opening day, 27 May, being caught too far forward between the river and the Chemin des Dames ridge to the north. By early June the Germans had achieved almost as deep a penetration as they had in 'Michael', their troops approaching to within 40 miles of Paris. Once again however, as in 1914, they were held on the River Marne. A two-pronged attack near Reims in mid-July, which brought only limited gains, marked the end of Ludendorff's attempts to bring the war to a conclusion with a clear victory on the Western Front.

3 The 8th Battalion during the German Offensive

The men of the 8th Battalion spent the first weeks of 1918 in the area of Houthulst Forest where they had seen out the old year after the Third Battle of Ypres had ended. In early February they left 1st Division, which had been their 'home' since the summer of 1915 and were allocated to 18th Division, taking the place in 53rd Brigade of the disbanded 6th Battalion of the Royal Berkshires, alongside the 7th Royal West Kents and the 10th Essex. 18th Division was then moved in mid-February to the southernmost sector of the British line between St Quentin and Noyon, recently taken over from the French and now held by Gough's Fifth Army.

The position occupied by the 8th Battalion on that part of the front was described by Lieutenant J W Randall, Platoon Commander of 'C' Company, in a memoir written in early September 1918 whilst he was convalescing after having been wounded in the opening days of the German offensive:

'We were holding a considerable front, some six miles south of St Quentin, with a battalion of the 14th Division on our left and a bat-

German troops in St Quentin, 19 March 1918 (IWM Q55479)

talion of our own brigade on the right – the Royal West Kents. At this point there was an unusual distance between our front line and that of the enemy, varying from 1,500 to 2,000 yards. The Canal de L'Oise et la Sambre ran between the lines, but small bridges over this were still in existence. There were also the ruins of two villages on the battalion front: – Alaincourt, facing our northern boundary and Moy, which was opposite the southern end of the sector. It was interesting to study these with binoculars, and in Moy the château and the railway station could be easily picked out. Our patrols used to go through the villages nightly, and they were very keen as the brigadier had offered 14 days' special leave to anyone who brought in a prisoner.'

Lieutenant-Colonel R E Dewing's battalion headquarters was close to La Guingette farm east of the village of Cerizy, north-west of Moy, and two companies, 'B' and 'D', were in the front line of the forward zone, close to Magpie Wood. 'A' Company was in support whilst 'C' Company was held in readiness behind the farm as the reserve and counter-attack unit. It was from the high ground around Magpie Wood that the men had the view over the German positions described by Lieutenant Randall.

For the night of 20 March a large-scale raid had been planned on the German trenches with the aim of bringing back prisoners. However, given by now the certainty, confirmed that day in an intelligence report circulated by Fifth Army headquarters, that the German offensive was imminent, the raid was cancelled. The day was used by 'C' Company

Sketch map of the 8th Battalion's positions on 21 March 1918 as included in the Battalion War Diary (PRO WO95/2037)

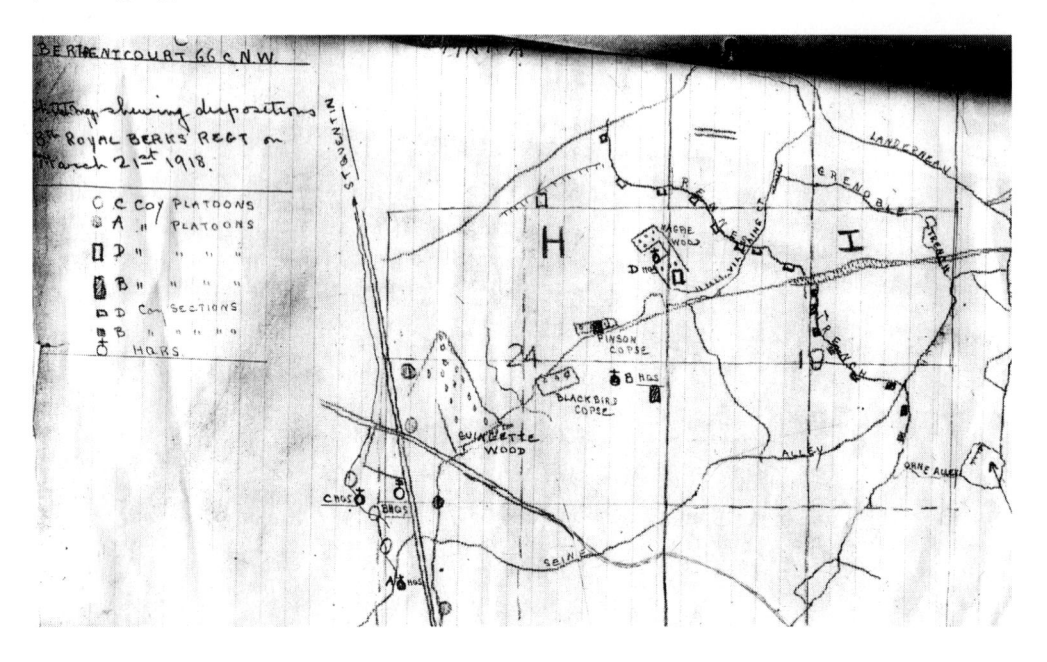

to reconnoitre the ground between their positions and the front line, on the assumption that they might have to be counter-attacking across it the next day. After dark, sentries were posted and the men were told to get as much rest as possible. Lieutenant Randall listened to their conversation:

> 'They were all perfectly cheerful and quite convinced that it was purely a case of "wind up". I heard my batman tell a little group that the latest rumour was that tomorrow the Huns were commencing a 10 years' bombardment, followed by four years of gas, "and then", he added, "They're coming over!"'

Opening of the German Offensive

At 4.40am on the following morning the German attack opened with a heavy barrage of shrapnel, high explosive and gas shells. As far as Lieutenant Randall was concerned,

> 'all we could do was to crouch low in the trench and pray hard that a shell would not land right amongst us ... it is impossible to describe the relief one felt when the shells no longer fell all around, and I know every man would have joyfully welcomed the approach of a million Huns to such a hell as we experienced during that six hours bombardment.'

News of the arrival of the Germans on the Royal Berkshires' front was brought to battalion headquarters by Lieutenant T H Baker, himself already badly wounded, at 10.00am. By this time all telephone communication with the forward companies had been broken, exacerbating the difficulties caused by the mist and the smoke from shell-bursts which hindered observation and made visual communication virtually impossible. Lieutenant Baker, before making his way back to the dressing station to have his facial wound attended, was able to report that the Germans had broken through on 'D' Company's front.

There was no news from 'B' Company. Two runners, Private H Butcher and Private G Sparrow, tried to get in touch with the front line, making their way through the barrage and towards 'D' Company headquarters in Magpie Wood. Before reaching the wood they met the enemy and had to turn back. It appeared from information given by men of 'A' Company in support that they had temporarily checked the German advance on their line at around 10.00am, but by 10.30am groups of the enemy were seen moving along the St Quentin-Moy road towards battalion headquarters.

In view of this threat, Lieutenant-Colonel Dewing ordered his headquarters staff to move further to the rear into 'C' Company's trench.

Captain H le G Sarchet stayed behind with the orderly room clerk, Sergeant H S Smith, to destroy secret papers. Whilst there they were attacked, but Captain Sarchet managed to dispose of several Germans with his revolver before leaving the dugout. Sergeant Smith took back with him some essential papers and in recognition of his gallantry and marked devotion to duty he was later awarded the Distinguished Conduct Medal.

Lieutenant Randall described the subsequent events:

> 'It was still impossible to see for more than 50 yards but we eventually saw a few German scouts loom out of the mist. These were promptly killed. Then appeared their first line of attackers, in extended order, at short intervals, and they came on very steadily and made an ugly rush. 'C' Company and its reinforcements were in great form however and not a man got within 20 yards of us.
> The men were greatly encouraged by the Colonel who walked up and down, cheering everyone up, and I heard him repeating: "Keep it up boys. There are rows and rows of dead Jerrys in front".'

But despite this resistance, other German units had worked their way round the battalion's position and were opening fire from all sides, using shell holes for cover. A particularly active sniper in one of these shell holes was located by Lieutenant N Williams who, accompanied by Private J E Peters, rushed the man, took him prisoner and was bringing him back in when he himself was shot and killed by a sniper. Another casualty was Captain H R Fenner, 'C' Company Commander, who was wounded in the head and taken prisoner.

With the German attackers being continually reinforced and with the remainder of his battalion virtually surrounded, Lieutenant-Colonel Dewing ordered a withdrawal down Seine Alley, a communication trench leading from the forward zone to the battle zone. The battalion now numbered fewer than 200 men, the rest having been killed or taken prisoner in the opening encounter. As they moved in single file down the trench they encountered a large party of Germans, armed with grenades, who had apparently been detailed to cut off the retreat. Lieutenant S A G Harvey who was leading the retirement shot the first German he met with his revolver but was killed himself simultaneously, according to the historian of the 18th Division, by the German officer he had shot. Major D Tosetti, second-in-command of the battalion, was also killed whilst attempting to silence a German machine gun.

The survivors, now under the temporary command of Sergeant W J Spokes, having carried on a running fight down Seine Alley reached the battle zone at about 1.30pm. Here they joined men of the 10th Essex who were holding a line assisted by a trench mortar unit and six Vickers machine guns. During the afternoon they made several unsuccessful attempts to get in touch with any units to the left or the right of them and by evening they had to rely on constant patrolling to prevent themselves being surprised by the enemy. At midnight Lieutenant-Colonel Dewing received orders to withdraw south-westwards through Rémigny across the St Quentin Canal towards Faillouel where he was to await further instructions.

The final details of this dramatic and very costly day's actions were recorded by Lieutenant Randall:

> 'It was highly desirable that the withdrawal should not be discovered by the enemy whilst it was actually in progress and the men were taken from the trench in small bodies and assembled just in the rear. A few sentries were kept in the line to fire occasional rifle shots while the assembly was taking place, and when the main body moved off they doubled after us and fell in at the rear of the column. It was a dark night and proceeding with the utmost caution we succeeded in avoiding the enemy and continued on our way without our withdrawal being discovered.'

On the morning of 22 March the men went into huts between Frières Faillouel and Faillouel, occupying a position on either side of the Frières Faillouel road late in the afternoon. The quarter-master had made a dump of the day's rations here, placed in sand-bags. These supplies had been drawn for a battalion fighting strength of about 600 men and so, as Lieutenant Randall notes, as they then numbered slightly over one hundred, practically every man received a sand-bag containing six times the normal ration, 'the meal of their army career'. Those who ate up the full allotment were the wise ones; a few hours later, in response to calls from other units, each man had to give up a portion of his share to feed the hungry.

Between 23 and 26 March the battalion, having received a draft of about 200 men under Major H B Morony, made a series of withdrawals, moving now almost due south, crossing the River Oise at Varesnes and moving on through Pontoise and down to Caisnes, well inside the area defended by the French army. From here they marched south-east to Nampcel where, from 26 March, the whole of 18th Division rested. On 27 March the division was placed in reserve, receiving orders on the following day to move north-westwards to the Amiens sector. This would mean a journey of some 24 hours, even by motor transport.

By now the remnants of the 8th Royal Berkshires and of the 7th Royal West Kents had been formed into a composite battalion under Lieutenant-Colonel Dewing. Together with the 53rd Trench Mortar Battery they totalled 23 officers and 433 other ranks. These figures compare with a battalion strength for the 8th Royal Berkshires on 21 March of 33 officers and 773 other ranks.

8th Battalion casualties for the period between 21 and 27 March were recorded as:

Officers killed
   Maj D Tosetti; Capt C A Birch; Lts S A G Harvey, N Williams; 2nd Lts E G King, J C Gordon (all on 21 March)

Officers wounded
   Lts T H Baker (21 March), H B F Kenney (25 March)
   2nd Lt J W Randall (24 March)

Officers missing
   Capts C H C Byrne, H R Fenner, D J Footman; Lts C F R Bland, G R Goodship, N Langston, E F Mecey;
   2nd Lts G Capes, W C A Hanney, W V Heale, E F Johnson, J R McMullen, T H Roberts, A G Williams (all on 21 March)

Other ranks
   19 killed; 37 wounded; 10 wounded and missing; 386 missing;
   1 missing believed killed

Total:
   23 officers and 453 other ranks

The total casualties for the period 21 March to 3 April (the day before the next major action involving the battalion) were:

   24 officers and 469 other ranks

These were the third highest casualties in 18th Division for the period, the officer casualties being the highest. Remembering these losses Lieutenant Randall concluded his memoir:

> 'The 8th Royal Berkshire Regiment has every reason to be proud of its efforts and sacrifices during these days, especially of their resistance on 21 March 1918, when they were bearing the brunt of attacks by two enemy divisions.'

Action at Hangard Wood 4 April

The next engagement of the 8th Battalion came on 4 April, during the defence of Amiens. It is worth pointing out that their billets at that time, in the village of Gentelles, were over 40 miles to the west of their positions on 21 March near Alaincourt and Moy. Their distance travelled had been of course considerably greater because of the deep arc they had traced to the south during their retreat. They were now eight miles south-east of Amiens in 53rd Brigade reserve and waiting to be called upon to counter an expected attack by German units through Hangard Wood. This butterfly-shaped wood lay (and lies today) in a slight hollow in the fields to the east of Gentelles, over a mile away. To the north-east was Villers-Bretonneux, later in the month to become the scene of bitter fighting when taken and then lost by the Germans.

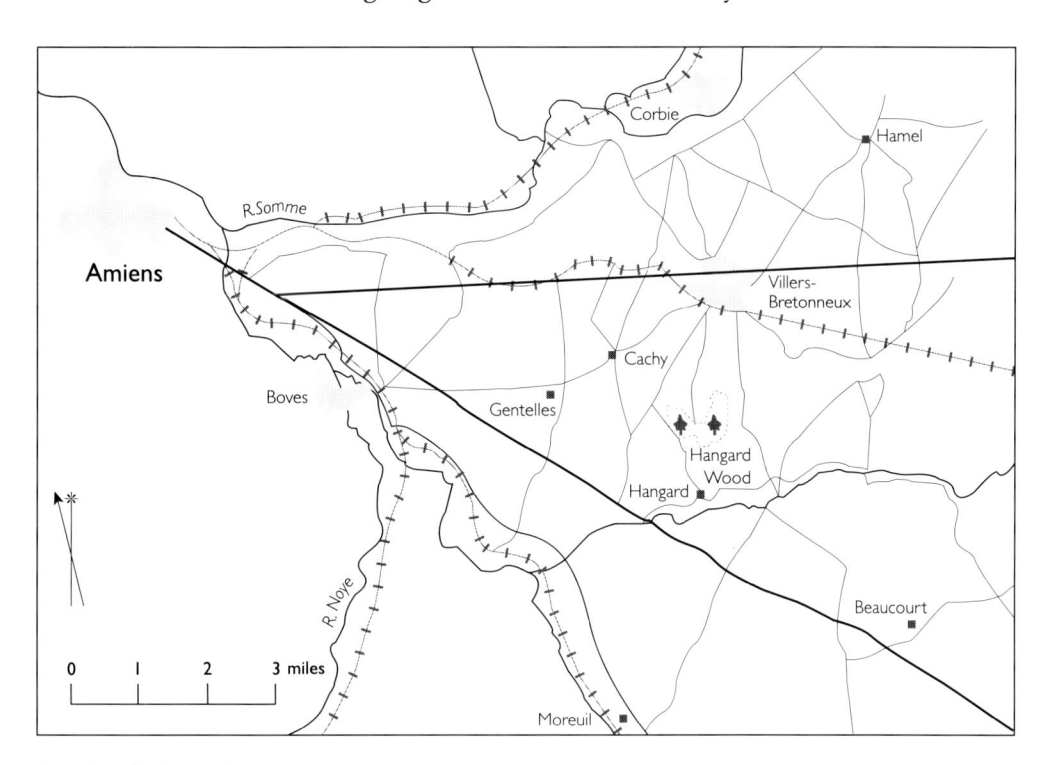

Area of the 8th Battalion's action on 4 April 1918

Gentelles was heavily shelled early in the morning of 4 April and at 10.00am, with an attack apparently imminent, the battalion was ordered to take up positions at the northern tip of Hangard Wood. It was not until 5.00pm that a strong enemy force was seen to be advancing in waves towards the wood. The 8th Battalion opened up with Lewis gun and rifle fire, causing heavy casualties, and they then went forward in counter-attack. At this point Lieutenant-Colonel Dewing was wounded in the leg and had to leave his headquarters. He was being carried to the rear by his servant, Private F Bailey, when a stray bullet struck him in the head, killing him instantaneously. Private Bailey was also hit but escaped serious injury. Almost at the same time the battalion adjutant, Captain H le G Sarchet, was seriously wounded. Before leaving his headquarters, Lieutenant-Colonel Dewing had given instructions to Captain R Holland about the deployment of the reserve company, but he too was killed.

Command of the battalion then devolved on Lieutenant A M Bray

The 8th Battalion during the German Offensive

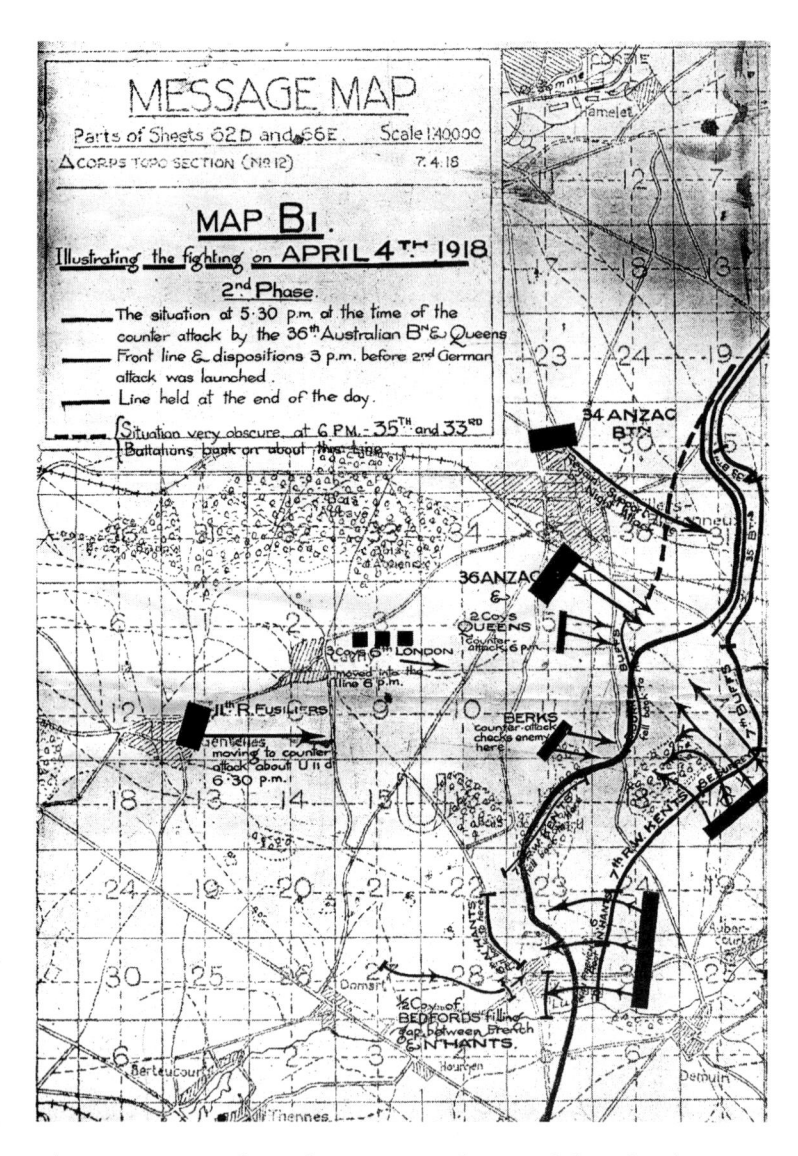

The 8th Battalion's counter-attack on 4 April 1918 (PRO WO95/2017)

who at 6.00pm, in face of superior numbers, withdrew headquarters some 600 yards to a point on the road between Hangard and Villers-Bretonneux. From this position the battalion's covering fire forced the enemy to break off the attack. Some ground had been lost, but part of Hangard Wood remained in British hands. What the historian of the 18th Division called 'the swift and deadly counter-attack' of the 8th Battalion had played a part in preventing a German breakthrough on ground which gave observation over Amiens and whose capture could have posed a threat to that city, a key point in the Allied line. Both the battalion's counter-attack and the death of Lieutenant-Colonel Dewing attracted a mention from the Official British Historian, J E Edmonds.

14   *Their Duty Done*

Casualties for the action on 4 April were recorded as:

Officers killed
   Lt-Col R E Dewing; Capt R Holland

Wounded and missing
   Capt H le G Sarchet (later recorded as killed)

Wounded
   Capt J M Richardson; 2nd Lts A W Morland, E Wallis

Other ranks
   3 killed; 1 wounded and missing; 39 wounded; 12 missing

Total:
   6 officers and 55 other ranks

Battalion strength before the action was, according to the regimental historian, between 250 and 300 other ranks.

On 5 April command of the battalion was briefly assumed by Major H B Morony. The following day they were relieved by units of the 5th Australian Brigade and they moved into billets, first in Gentelles and then in St Nicolas, two miles to the west. On 10 April, whilst the battalion was in Boves, Major T M Banks of the 10th Essex Regiment took command. He was replaced later in the month by Captain (Acting Lieutenant-Colonel) N B Hudson, brother of Captain A H Hudson killed on 31 July 1917 at Ypres with the 6th Battalion and of Captain T H Hudson killed on 13 October 1915 at Loos with the 5th Battalion. By this time the battalion had been re-fitted and was training new drafts of 16 officers and 589 other ranks who had come in from other units.

After a spell 'on loan' to 8th Division they returned to 18th Division on 26 April and went into billets. The German offensive on this front had by now come to a standstill and the battalion was able to enjoy what the regimental historian calls 'a long period of comparative rest after the terrible weeks succeeding the 21st March'.

4 The 5th Battalion during the German Offensive

The men of the 5th Battalion, unlike their colleagues in the 8th, were not directly involved on the opening day of the German offensive. At the beginning of 1918, their division, the 12th, had moved out of the rest area where they had been since the Battle of Cambrai, and had gone into the line near Merville on the River Lys. Here in a quiet sector, on marshy, low-lying ground, was a rather dilapidated trench system where the front line consisted for the most part merely of outposts and where the main activity for both sides was raiding.

Private Harry Harding of Reading, who served with the battalion throughout the war, made a laconic reference in a post-war memoir to his time here: 'January 1918 in and out of the Fleur Bay (Fleurbaix) and Laventy (Laventie) sectors. All mud and breastworks, where the daily phut of gas shells was a danger.'

In early February the 5th Battalion was moved from 35th to 36th Brigade of 12th Division, as part of that general reorganisation of the BEF which had brought about the demise of the 6th Battalion. In 36th Brigade with them were the 9th Royal Fusiliers and the 7th Royal Sussex. From now on, German preparations for the forthcoming offensive began to make themselves felt in this sector too. There was an increase in artillery fire, with roads and back areas included in the heavy shelling. On 21 March the line from Laventie to Armentières was subjected to gas shelling, the German intention being to suggest that an attack here was imminent and thus to forestall any dispatch of British troops to the south. In the event, on 24 March 12th Division was sent by motor transport down to the Somme area where they found themselves on the following day west of Albert and awaiting further orders.

At 4.30pm on 25 March the Royal Berkshires went forward with 36th Brigade to occupy a line from Montauban to Bazentin-le-Grand, familiar names of the 1916 campaign. An hour later they were ordered to Montauban in support of another division but were diverted back to Albert, and by 4.30am on the following day – following a night of marching and waiting for further orders – they had taken up a position on the western bank of the Ancre River where 12th Division was to hold a line from Albert to Hamel. When 36th Brigade had established itself here, the 5th Battalion went into reserve at Martinsart, holding a line along a railway embankment just east of the village behind Aveluy Wood. The historian of the 12th Division described the difficulties of defending this sector:

> 'There were no trenches, and so the natural line of resistance for the greater portion of the front became the railway embankment, wherever it was suitable. The lack of entrenching tools was now severely felt, as any scraps of old trenches still in existence were quite useless. The Division had no hand or rifle grenades, no Verey lights or means of communicating SOS signals, and there was no defensive wire. In this condition the German attack was awaited.'

The 5th Battalion spent 26 March in reconnoitring positions around Martinsart but early on the following morning, when a German attack seemed to be in progress from the north, one company took up posi-

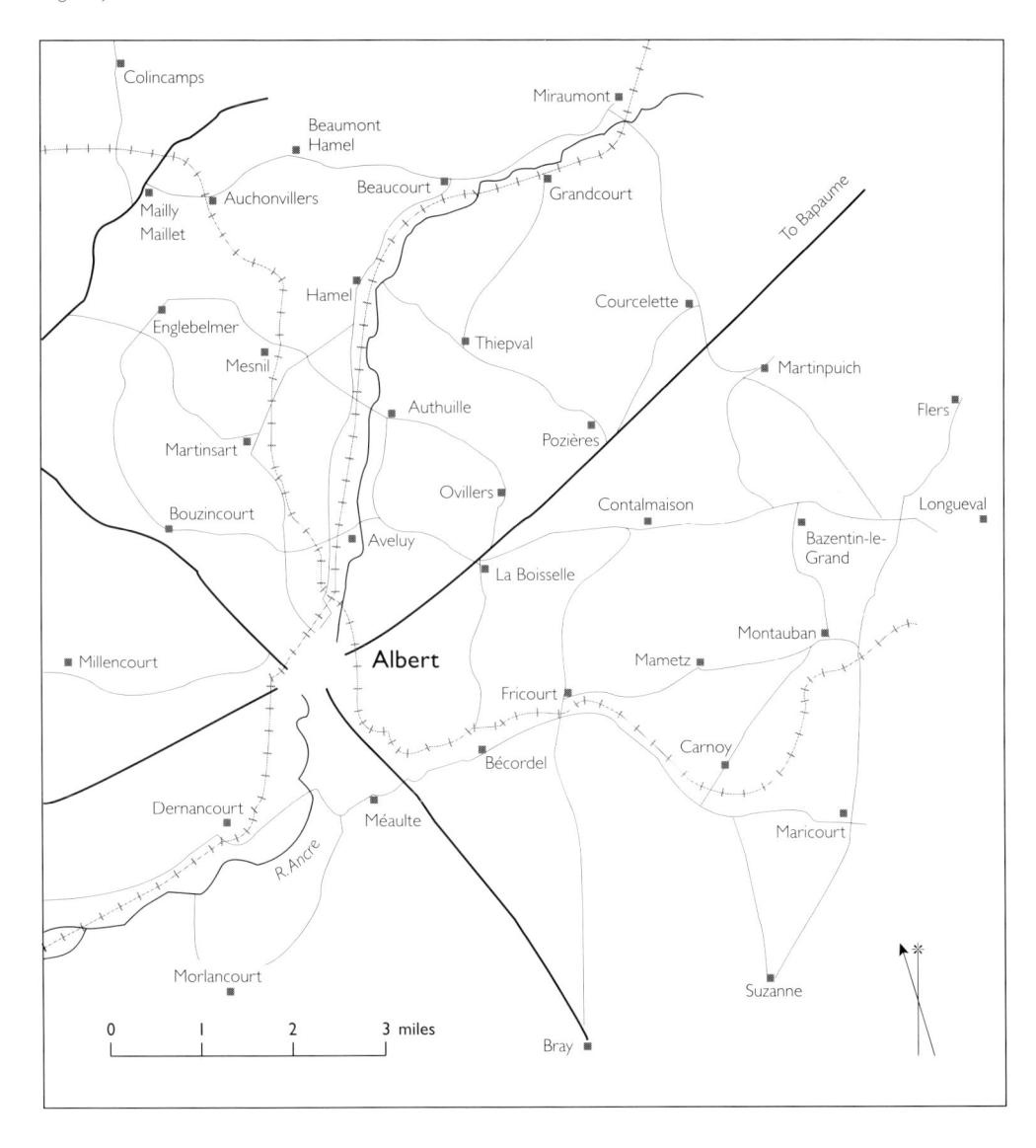

Area of the 5th Battalion's actions in March, April and August 1918

The 5th Battalion during the German Offensive

tion to cover Martinsart village whilst two others were sent to help 37th Brigade. One of these companies moved through Aveluy Wood at 3.00am to clear it of the enemy but they did not encounter any German troops. A platoon of the company covering Martinsart however saw German troops moving along the road to Mesnil, opened fire with rifles and Lewis guns and forced them into cover, from where they were driven back by a battalion of the Royal Naval Division.

Between 3.00pm and 4.00pm the Officer Commanding the 5th Battalion, Lieutenant-Colonel E H J Nicolls, received instructions to alter his disposition so as to face south, as an enemy attack was threatened from that direction. To help stem this attack he sent 'A' Company to fill a gap which had opened between the two other battalions in the brigade. The men were held up by heavy machine gun fire from the direction of Aveluy and both the Company Commander and his Second-in-Command were killed. At 5.00pm the Germans again attacked in force from the south and south-east, this time supported by low-flying aircraft. They broke through the outpost line and the front line and penetrated as far as the support and reserve lines on the 36th Brigade front. The defence of the sector had now to be reorganised and the 5th Battalion took up a position on a ridge just south of the wood at Martinsart.

At 9.00am on 28 March another strong German force attacked from Aveluy. The British artillery brought down a heavy barrage on Aveluy Ridge and two companies of the 5th Battalion and units of the 9th Royal Fusiliers combined to force the Germans back with rifle and machine gun fire. Considerable casualties were inflicted and the enemy were seen to carry their wounded back across the Ancre River and up the slope towards La Boisselle.

This was the last engagement for the Royal Berkshires on this sector. In the early hours of 29 March the battalion was relieved by the 6th Royal West Kents and marched into rest in Warloy west of Albert. As the historian of the 12th Division put it: 'A day or two to clean themselves and get a few hours unmolested sleep was greatly appreciated by the troops.'

Casualties were reported as:

Officers killed
  2nd Lt J H Matthews

Officers died of wounds
  Capt G G Paine

Officers wounded
  Capt E H Lloyd, Lt J S Noble

Other ranks
    10 killed 65 wounded

On 15 April awards for gallantry during these actions were made:

Military Cross to
    2nd Lt T P Meyrick

Military Medal to
    Cpl R McAllister, Pte G Jackson

A reminder of the continuing problem of communication in battle was given in the 36th Brigade War Diary for this period which stated that operations had been considerably hampered by lack of telephone cables. Visual signalling had been a partial replacement but no pigeons had been available. Reliance on runners had meant that the artillery had on occasion been slow in opening fire.

Mark V tanks of the 2nd Tank Battalion halted in Aveluy. On the road are also transport limbers. 25 March 1918 (IWM Q8639)

The 5th Battalion during the German Offensive

Action west of Albert

The 5th Battalion's second spell of action during the German offensive started barely five days later when 12th Division was sent into the line on the night of 2 April. The division was now due west of Albert, holding a sector of some 4,000 yards, with an Australian division on their right. The Germans attacked the Australians twice on 3 April, without success, but there was no action on the Royal Berkshires' front. The following afternoon, after a brief but intense artillery barrage, German units attempted to rush trenches held by neighbouring battalions. Lewis gunners of the 5th Battalion helped to beat off the attack.

During the night of 4 April messages from French General Headquarters indicated a probable enemy attack in strength the next day. At 7.00am on 5 April the whole of 12th Division's front was shelled, with back areas being subjected to gas. First attacks at 7.30am were repulsed but a second attack at 9.30am penetrated the 5th Battalion's line. After fierce fighting the Germans were ejected, as the battalion diarist put it: 'with the help of the 9th Royal Fusiliers'. The historian of the 12th Division is by omission less complimentary to the Royal Berkshires. He states: 'They (the Germans) were ejected by a successful counter-attack delivered by the 9th Royal Fusiliers.'

A further German attack at 12 noon did succeed in denting the battalion's line and a copse was taken. In an attempt to regain the lost ground, men of the reserve company were brought up at 2.30pm. Their advance took them up a slope exposed to intense enemy machine gun fire and here they lost half their strength, their casualties including the Company Commander, Captain J R West MC. They managed to reach the line of their old support trench and dug in, but they could not re-take the copse. The officer who took over command from Captain West and led the remainder of the company to their final position was Second Lieutenant I R Baird who was subsequently awarded the Military Cross for conspicuous gallantry and devotion to duty. In the words of the official citation:

> 'He immediately took charge, rallied the survivors and reached the objective. Finding the line disorganised, he immediately systematised the defence and by his prompt action succeeded in repelling the attack.'

Casualties in the 5th Battalion had been so heavy in the fighting of 5 April that when, at 4.00pm on the following day, they came out of the line, they had to be reorganised into just two companies, each placed at the disposal of another battalion. Their own battalion trench strength was a mere 231, official returns for the full battalion strength at the beginning of the day having been 33 officers and 683 other ranks.

Casualties were reported as:

Officers wounded
> Capts L Fenton, D E Ward, J R West; Lt A G Punnett;
> 2nd Lts H S Handley, C A Nott, J F W Shedel

Officers missing
> 2nd Lts W Barker, B Miles, H E Palmer, A Waite, C A Wilmshurst

Other ranks
> 243 killed, wounded and missing

On 21 April awards for gallantry displayed on 5 April were made:

Military Cross to
> 2nd Lt I R Baird

Military Medal to
> Cpl F Varney; L/Cpls J Gurr (bar), H Littlefield, W Kent; Pte H Furber

On 7 April the battalion moved into billets in Hénencourt, by which time the German offensive on Somme front had been brought to a halt.

Trench raid at Hamel

The one remaining episode of front line action experienced by the 5th Battalion before the Allied armies went over to the offensive came on 24/25 May, when they were in the line facing Hamel, west of the River Ancre near Beaucourt. They were called upon to mount a large-scale night trench raid in co-operation with the Anson Battalion of the Royal Naval Division. Two companies were to occupy the German front line and consolidate it to cover the return at the end of the raid, whilst two following companies were to pass through into the German support trenches, search them and bring back prisoners.

From a report on the raid written on 29 May by Major H T Goodland and lodged with the Battalion War Diary the following graphic picture emerges:

After a certain amount of confusion caused by an enemy barrage in No Man's Land just after zero hour (11.15pm) which caused heavy casualties, the two leading companies advanced according to plan and captured all their objectives. One of the following companies lost direction and contact with the Anson Battalion was also lost. Two platoons reached their part of their objective but, not being in touch with one another or with the Royal Naval Division, they did not go further. At zero plus 1 hour 25 minutes reports were received that the task had been completed as far as was possible and a satisfactory withdrawal was then carried out. Communication throughout the raid was bad, only runners could be used forward of battalion headquarters, and it took an hour to get a message from the Anson Battalion.

One passage in Major Goodland's report reveals the nature of this kind of operation:

> 'Hostile infantry showed very little fight, except from dug-outs, when they fired automatic pistols up the steps. One German put his hands up and when our man advanced towards him, he tried to stab him with a dagger which he had concealed in his hand. He was dealt with accordingly. A few prisoners showed fight and refused to come in and so had to be killed.'

Despite the problems encountered, 21 prisoners and five machine guns were brought in. An estimated 50 Germans were killed during the raid.

5th Battalion casualties were reported as:

Officers wounded

Lt E J Joseph; 2nd Lts I R Baird, D H Betts, T H Eayrs

Other ranks

12 killed; 2 died of wounds; 73 wounded; 19 missing

Trench map included in the Battalion War Diary showing German positions in the raid on May 24/25 1918 (PRO W095/1856)

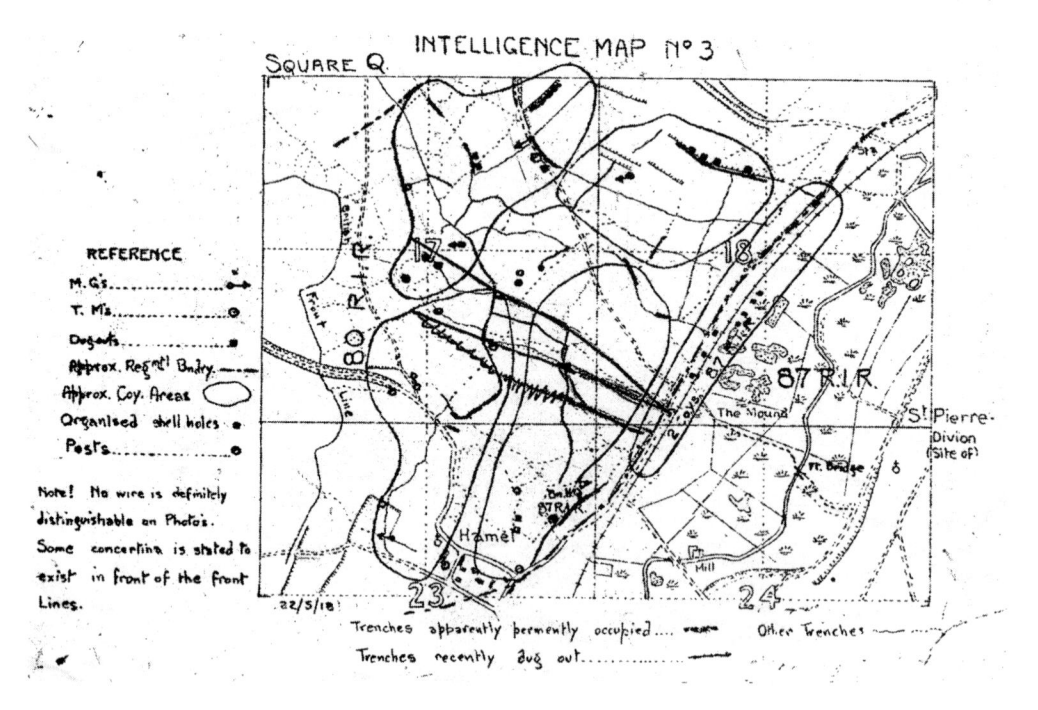

As far as the historian of the 12th Division was concerned, the operation, very carefully rehearsed, 'proved very successful.' Congratulations, he noted, were received from the Army and Corps Commanders. Picked out for special mention were Corporal J J Sargeant for displaying conspicuous bravery in dealing with dug-outs, and Lance-Corporal C Gale who distinguished himself in capturing a machine gun. The praise carries all the more weight when set against the statement in a preliminary report on the raid submitted to 36th Brigade under the heading Lessons Learnt: 'With a battalion consisting chiefly of raw drafts, more preliminary training is necessary.'

With the German Spring Offensives now effectively at an end on this part of the front, the 5th Battalion remained in the sector north of the River Somme throughout June and July, taking spells in the front line and spending periods in reserve.

5 Final Allied Offensive

By mid-July 1918 the Ludendorff offensives had clearly failed to achieve any strategic results. A joint French and American counter-attack in the south, launched by General Mangin on 18 July, then heralded the start of a succession of Allied attacks which were eventually to bring the war to a conclusion.

Earlier in July, a relatively minor action at Le Hamel, north-east of Villers-Bretonneux, fought by the Australian Corps under General Monash, had shown what could now be accomplished by close co-operation between artillery, machine guns, tanks, aircraft and infantry. Thoroughly prepared, the attack was designed to pinch out a small German salient and thus straighten the Australian line in anticipation of a later offensive. The 4th Australian Division together with a contingent of American troops went forward close up behind a creeping barrage, supported by 60 British tanks, and within an hour and a half all objectives, including the village itself, had been taken, as had some 1,500 German prisoners.

The tactics of Le Hamel were then employed on a much larger scale east of Amiens on 8 August. Here at 4.20am 11 divisions of Rawlinson's Fourth Army, including the Australian Corps and the fresh Canadian Corps (brought into the line under great secrecy), launched a surprise attack on a 13-mile front with the support of over 400 tanks and 800 aircraft. French forces attacked on a 7-mile front to their right. Opposing them were 14 German divisions whose capacity for tough resistance had been estimated by Allied intelligence as doubtful and whose defensive positions were poorly maintained.

This Allied offensive, as had its German counterpart on 21 March, opened in thick mist. Tanks operating on favourable ground, an effective creeping barrage and the use of reserves to 'leap-frog' the attacking infantry were significant ingredients in the achievement of a 7-mile advance and the capture of some 15,000 prisoners. A feature of the operation was the performance of the tanks. The new Mark V was a more powerful and reliable machine than its immediate predecessor and the smaller, faster 'Whippets' and armoured cars were able to cause considerable damage behind the German lines.

The one major disappointment of the day was the inability of the British divisions north of the Somme to take all their objectives and thus fully secure the Australians' left flank. In one of these divisions, the 18th, both Royal Berkshire battalions were at that time serving. The troops had been heavily involved in the fighting earlier in the year and were perhaps battle-weary. They had also been subjected to a surprise German attack two days before the Allied offensive opened. However, at the Battle of Amiens a significant victory was won and General Ludendorff was famously to declare 8 August as the 'black day' of the German army in the history of the war.

On the following day, Australian and Canadian units made a 3-mile advance south of the Somme. By this time, of the 430 tanks in action on 8 August, only 155 were still usable, and battlefield communication was now much more of a problem in the open warfare which followed the initial advance. The Germans had also had time to bring up reinforcements and the Allied attacks on this front were effectively halted on 11 August having achieved a limited, but promising tactical success.

Allied strategy was now to keep up the momentum of the offensive by switching the point of attack and not allowing time for the German forces to re-group. Between 21 August and 25 September, separate attacks by the British First, Third and Fourth Armies took the advance to within 14 miles of the Hindenburg Line. This formidable position stretching from Cambrai to La Fère was in places 10 miles deep and consisted of a number of defensive lines protected by deep belts of wire entanglements and concrete emplacements. Between Cambrai and St Quentin the main Hindenburg system took in the Canal du Nord, at this time dry, and the St Quentin Canal.

The northern extension of the Hindenburg Line, known to the Allies as the Drocourt-Quéant Switch Line, was taken by the Canadian Corps on 2 September. This caused the German High Command to order a large-scale withdrawal, in effect giving up the remainder of the territory won in the March and April offensives. An attack against the Canal du Nord on 27 September by First and Third Armies made a breach of 12 miles wide and six miles deep in this section of the Hindenburg Line.

This success was followed up two days later by British, Australian and American units of Fourth Army attacking on a 12-mile front north of St Quentin. It was here that men of the 46th (North Midland) Division had the honour of leading the crossing of the St Quentin Canal near Bellenglise – supported, literally, by 3,000 lifebelts borrowed from Channel steamers. On this front an advance of over three miles had been accomplished at relatively light cost. It is no coincidence that on 29 September the German High Command informed the Kaiser that the war could not be won and that Germany must ask for an armistice.

The final stages of the Allied offensive involved Second Army in the north attacking on 28 September to regain the ridges around Ypres. Then followed a crossing of the River Lys on 19 October and a subsequent advance taking in Tourcoing and Roubaix and beyond them the line of the River Scheldt. The Fifth Army on their right took Lille and

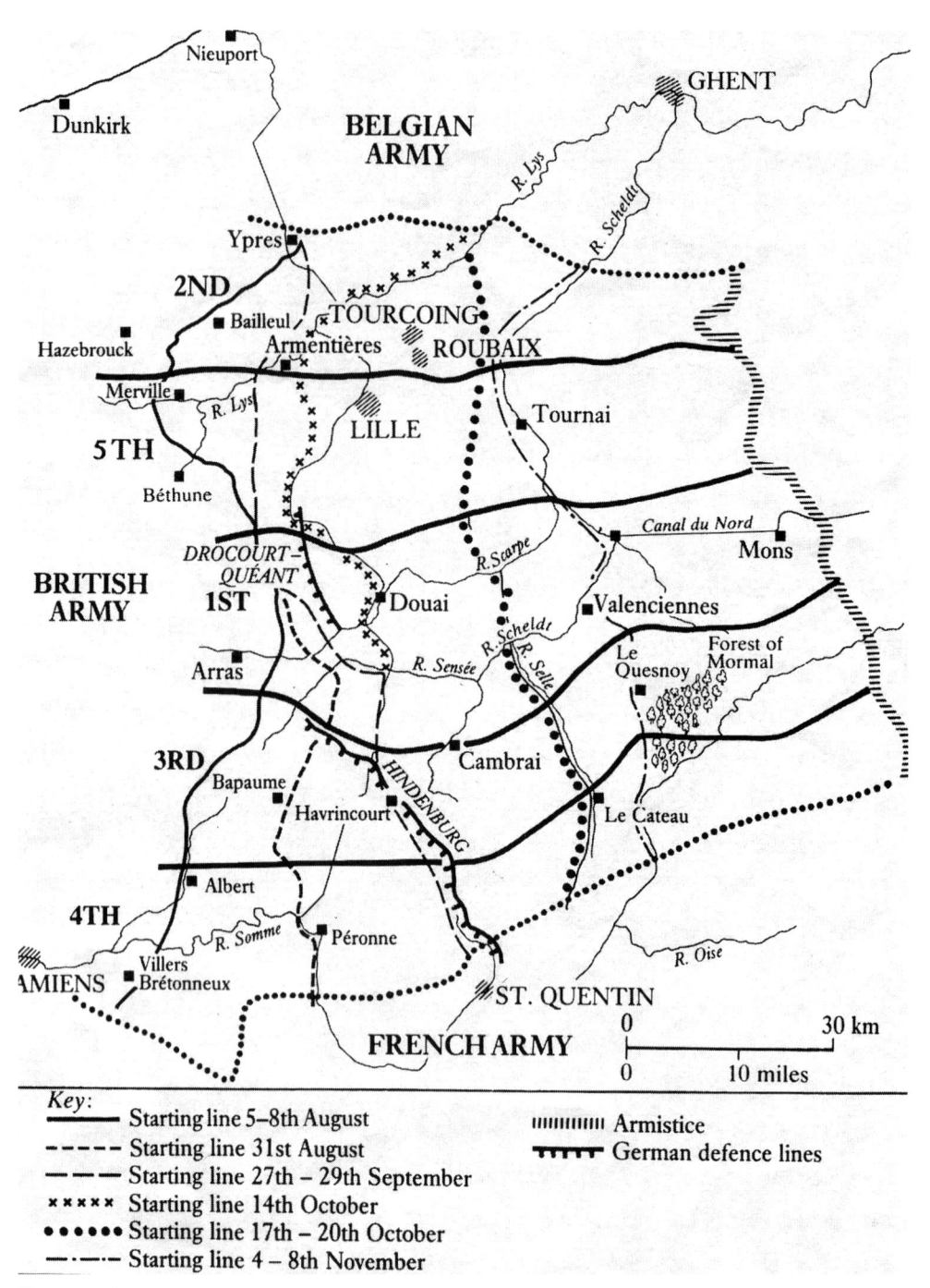

The Allied advance to victory
8 August–11 November 1918
(Reproduced by kind permission of Polity Press from Trevor Wilson, The Myriad Faces of War, 1986)

Their Duty Done

Tournai. Further south, the line of the River Selle was forced in late October, bringing names familiar from the days of 1914 back into the operation orders, among them Le Cateau and the Forest of Mormal. By the time that negotiations between the powers had been completed and the armistice agreement signed on 11 November, British and Dominion forces had reached Mons, where the BEF's first encounter with the German army had taken place four years earlier.

Pursuit to the River Selle. Troops going forward by Albion lorry, near Joncourt (captured 1 October). Gunners pulling 18-pounder out of ditch at roadside.
9 October 1918
(IWM Q9527)

Final Allied Offensive

6 The Battle of Amiens

The Battle of Amiens is notable not only for having brought about the 'black day of the German army' but also for marking the start of the series of Allied attacks which led to victory. For the two Kitchener battalions of the Royal Berkshire Regiment it was a unique occasion: for the first and only time in the war – and quite by chance – they served in the same division.

The main objective of the Allied attack on 8 August 1918 was to take the German-held outer defences of Amiens and make the town safe from bombardment. This would involve an average advance along the whole front of over 10,000 yards. North of the Somme, where the Royal Berkshire battalions were engaged, III Corps of Fourth Army was to establish a strong left flank by the capture of high ground south of the village of Morlancourt, including the Chipilly spur.

In contrast to the good campaigning country south of the river where the main attack by the Canadians and the Australians was to be made, the terrain here was much less favourable. Although the German defences in this sector were not in themselves a formidable obstacle, consisting as they did mainly of roughly-dug trenches and outposts, the ground was broken by deep ravines running from the Somme and the Ancre valleys and was vulnerable to enemy fire from the slopes of the Chipilly spur in the bend of the Somme. Prominent features were Malard Wood and Gressaire Wood. Because of the nature of the ground, the attack in this sector was, after the initial assault, to be con-

Battle of Amiens. Blown-up bridges across the Somme at Chipilly. 10 August 1918 (IWM Q6941)

Their Duty Done

ducted independently of the main attack to the south and its objectives for the first day were to be more limited.

Two days before the offensive was due to open, the Germans mounted a surprise attack on that part of III Corps line held by 18th Division, making a penetration of some 1,000 yards on the Bray-Corbie road and taking 200 prisoners. Most of this ground was re-taken on the following day, but it was the effect of the attack on the British troop deployment which was more serious. A brigade relief was in progress at the time and the brigade most affected, the 54th, had to be withdrawn from the line. In its place came 36th Brigade from 12th Division which was due to make its own attack north of 18th Division, a gap of some 500 yards having been left between the two divisions. With 36th Brigade came the 5th Royal Berkshires whose task would be to defend the left flank of 53rd Brigade. The 8th Royal Berkshires would thus fortuitously have the assistance of their regimental colleagues as they advanced.

8th Battalion attack

The first objective of 18th Division was a line east of Malard Wood running back across the Bray-Corbie road to the point where the British front was being held static. A second wave consisting of 53rd Brigade's battalions – the 7th Royal West Kents, the 10th Essex and the 8th Royal Berkshires – would then pass through to the final objective which took in the greater part of Gressaire Wood and a feature known as the Brickyard. This would entail an advance of some 4,000 yards and would secure the high ground on the Bray-Corbie ridge.

The whole of the attack on 8 August had been prepared in great secrecy. Brigade and Battalion Commanders were informed of the general plan only five days in advance and the front-line troops were told of their objectives only 36 hours before zero. As for the Battle of Cambrai in November 1917, there was to be no preliminary bombardment. At 4.20am, an hour before sunrise, infantry and tanks were to move forward together under a creeping barrage which would be put down by a third of the guns available. The remaining two-thirds would be engaged in counter-battery work, suppressing the German artillery.

All went according to plan, but the start for the troops of 18th Division was not easy. There was confusion in the heavy ground mist and progress by compass bearing was slow. The two companies of tanks allotted to the division failed to appear and the infantry had to make their assault unaided. The first objective was taken only when the 10th Essex of the second 'wave' leap-frogged through the battalions of the first and then pressed on, guided by the line of the Bray-Corbie

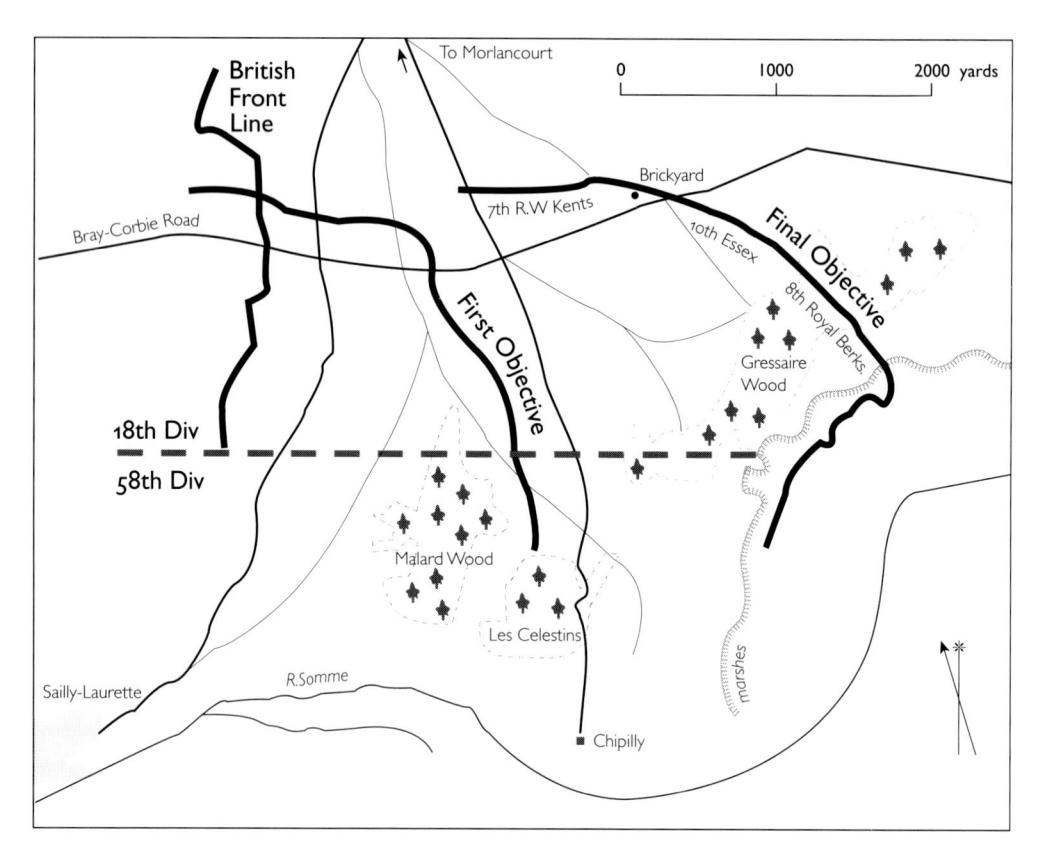

The 18th Division's attack front on 8 August 1918

road, and left the battalions behind to consolidate.

The 10th Essex, now reduced to fewer than a hundred men, reached the final objective by 7.20am and were then joined on their left flank by what were by then the remnants of the 7th West Kents. Missing at this stage were the 8th Royal Berkshires who should have taken the southern part of Gressaire Wood. After reconnoitring, the Commanding Officer of the 10th Essex, Lieutenant-Colonel Banks, became aware that German troops were still in the wood, that his right flank was therefore exposed and also that there was fighting going on behind him.

What the historian of the 18th Division called 'the young lads of the Berks' had come up without their tanks, finding direction in the mist by following the trampled paths in the grass and the corn made by the first wave. By 8.00am they had crossed a ravine leading down to the River Somme and the weather began to clear. Without warning they found themselves facing six German machine guns supported by two field guns firing over open sights at 500 yards range from Gressaire Wood.

Lieutenant-Colonel N B Hudson, who had assumed command of the battalion in April, then led one of three unsuccessful charges on the guns. At a distance of ten yards he was hit five times in the legs and body. He managed to scramble back behind the shelter of a bank where his men attended to him. By this time the mist had completely cleared and the German machine gunners brought down heavy fire on the battalion's position at the western edge of the wood. The Royal Berkshires managed to hold out here for forty minutes after Colonel Hudson had been taken back by his orderly, but at 9.00am they had to retire to the line of the first objective. Major SW Warr then took over command of the battalion.

Three hours later the 10th Essex were also forced to withdraw to the first objective line and it was here that the day's fighting ended for 18th Division. Although Gressaire Wood had not been taken, the high ground along the Bray-Corbie road had been kept out of enemy hands. To that extent, the objective of protecting the advance of the main body of troops south of the river had been at least partially achieved. In the evening the 8th Battalion was withdrawn for reorganisation.

Three companies of the 5th Battalion meanwhile, who under Captain A G Revell had moved off to their objective at 11.15am, had been able to consolidate their position on the Bray-Corbie road by 2.30pm from where they were relieved in the evening. Their Battalion War Diary makes no mention of any involvement in action or of any casualties on this day, nor does the regimental historian. The Battalion Commander, Lieutenant-Colonel H T Goodland, was however awarded the Distinguished Service Order for his conduct on that day, the official citation reading:

> 'For conspicuous gallantry, coolness and devotion to duty. He led his battalion, which had been in reserve, through a heavy enemy barrage to reinforce the firing line, and by so doing filled up a dangerous gap and stopped the advance of the enemy. He then personally supervised the consolidation of a vital position under direct fire from machine gun and field guns firing with open sights.'

In contrast, losses suffered by the 8th Battalion on 8 August were heavy. Officer casualties were given by the regimental historian as:

Killed
   Lt E M Hartree; 2nd Lt C W Moss

Died of wounds
   Lt A M Bray

Wounded
   Lt-Col N B Hudson; Capt C G M Morris; Lt A L Oliver;
   2nd Lts W C Molland, T Starbuck

In the course of the next two days the 8th Battalion moved back into the old German front line and there relieved the 5th Battalion before going briefly into shelter west of Albert.

The totals of other ranks casualties for the period 8–10 August, as submitted to 53rd Brigade, were:

> 21 killed, 83 wounded, 10 wounded & missing, 53 missing

Battalion strength before the action was 22 officers and 636 other ranks.

In recognition of his conduct on 8 August, Lieutenant-Colonel Hudson, who in 1917 whilst serving with the 6th Battalion had won the Military Cross & Bar, was awarded the Distinguished Service Order, the citation in the London Gazette of 4 October 1919 reading:

> 'For consistent gallantry and able leadership particularly on 8 August 1918, south of Morlancourt when he personally led his battalion forward to the attack through heavy fog and intense shell and machine gun fire. When they were held up by machine guns he pushed forward alone, knocking out one machine gun and getting wounded in doing so. In spite of this, he rushed two other machine guns which were holding up the advance and continued to lead his battalion forward until he was again seriously wounded by machine gun fire in three places. He showed splendid courage and determination.'

One sad footnote to these actions in the early days of August is the story of Private John Swain. Private Swain enlisted in the RAMC, was transferred to the 6th Battalion of the Royal Berkshire Regiment and on their disbandment went to the 5th Battalion. He was shot for desertion on 11 August and was buried in Montigny Communal Cemetery north-east of Corbie. There, as if to emphasise his separation from his comrades, his headstone stands alone.

Headstone of Private John Swain in Montigny Communal Cemetery Extension

7 The advance to Péronne

In the second phase of the final Allied offensive the two Royal Berkshire battalions again found themselves attacking side by side, although on this occasion each within its own division. The 12th and 18th Divisions were operating in late August to the north of the River Somme as part of Fourth Army's thrust eastwards from Albert which by the end of the month would take it to the outskirts of Péronne.

The immediate objective of the resumed advance, scheduled for 22 August and involving both divisions, was to secure the high ground north of the village of Bray-sur-Somme. For units of 12th Division, including the 5th Royal Berkshires, this meant capturing the village of Méaulte and securing a position along the Bray-Albert road to the south-east. Immediately to the north of them, 18th Division had the task of crossing the Ancre River north of Dernancourt and clearing the town of Albert. For this first part of the operation the 8th Royal Berkshires were in divisional reserve with 53rd Brigade. Their turn for action would come some days later.

5th Battalion at Méaulte

Zero on 22 August was at 4.45am. As at the Battle of Amiens, there was to be no preliminary bombardment; infantry and tanks were to move forward 200 yards behind the barrage which would lift 100 yards every four minutes, except on the 5th Battalion's front where the lifts would be every two minutes. A smoke screen was put down on the high ground which formed the objective in order to hinder enemy observation. It was also arranged that a contact aircraft would fly over at zero plus three hours and 15 minutes and that the infantry would signal their position by burning flares and displaying discs.

The troops of 12th Division, supported by 10 Mark V tanks, made good progress against not very strong opposition and by 6.45am their intermediate objective some 2000 yards from the starting line had been taken. Here the barrage halted for ten minutes and then, when the attack was resumed, three companies of the 5th Royal Berkshires cleared the whole of Méaulte and secured the high ground along the Bray-Albert road. During this action Lance-Sergeant E C Harvey's platoon was held up by a German machine gun. He rushed the gun, killing one man and forcing the rest of the team to surrender. For this and a

Mark V tanks of the 4th Tank Battalion in Méaulte soon after its capture by the 5th Battalion Royal Berkshire Regiment of the 12th Division. 22 August 1918 (IWM Q7302)

subsequent act of bravery Lance-Sergeant Harvey was awarded the Distinguished Conduct Medal.

In taking the village the men of the 5th Battalion were supported by four tanks, one of which moved up the main street whilst the others worked round on either side and dealt with German machine gun nests. An after-action report of the 4th Tank Battalion described the section of tanks as going ahead of the infantry and leading them through the village. The Tank Corps War Diary supports this account, referring to the day's fighting as a whole:

> 'The tanks were intended to go behind the infantry, but they actually found themselves fighting with, or in front of, the infantry the whole way'.

Instructions concerning infantry-tank cooperation set out in a paper included in the 36th Brigade War Diary for August 1918 have in this context an ironic ring:

> 'One intelligent infantryman will be detailed to travel in each fighting tank for the purpose of liaison between the crew and the infantry operating in the neighbourhood.'

The scene of this successful action at Méaulte was captured on camera by official photographers: a rare, if not unique, occurrence for a

Kitchener battalion of the Royal Berkshire Regiment.
5th Battalion casualties for 22 August were reported as:

Officers wounded

Capt J N Gregory; Lt E A Engelbach;
2nd Lts L Chapman, S M Eccles, C A Farebrother, L C Oakes

Other ranks

3 killed, 72 wounded

The 4th Tank Battalion reported two other ranks as slightly wounded, both of whom remained on duty.

Two men of the 12th Division taking cover behind a wall from splinters of a bursting shell. Méaulte, 23 August 1918 (IWM Q7089)

8th Battalion at La Boisselle

Meanwhile 18th Division had had the more difficult task of taking Albert, whose cellars offered the Germans excellent defensive positions, and of crossing the Ancre River, where all the bridges had been destroyed. The 8th Royal Berkshires did not take part in this action, nor in the one on 23 August, when they acted as support for the successful 53rd Brigade attack on another objective familiar from the 1916 Somme campaign: the Tara Hill-Usna Hill ridge west of La Boisselle.

The advance to Péronne

With the weather perfect it was decided at Fourth Army headquarters to keep up the momentum of the advance by launching a night attack so that advantage could be taken of a clear sky and a full moon. A 1.00am start on 24 August was chosen and 53rd Brigade were given the task, in cooperation with units of 38th Division, of taking the Chapes Spur running south from La Boisselle to Bécourt and Bécourt Wood. By 5.00am the Spur had been captured and a defensive flank formed facing south.

By 5.15am the 8th Battalion were reporting that they had reached their objectives but that a gap of some 200 yards between 'A' Company on the left and 'C' Company in the centre could not be closed because the enemy were holding on to the old British craters at La Boisselle. From here the Germans were sniping and putting their machine guns to very effective use.

A stalemate resulted which lasted for the rest of the day, but what followed in the evening caused the historian of the 18th Division later to assert that:

> 'The 24th of August 1918 ought always to be remembered in 18th Divisional history for the magnificent bit of individualism by which the 8th Royal Berkshires drove the Germans out of the notorious La Boisselle crater'.

At 8.00pm, under cover of a mortar bombardment, Second Lieutenants N H G Blackburn and T C Halliburton, acting under the orders of their respective Company Commanders, Lieutenant T K Pickard and Captain G W H Nicholson, led 60 men of 'A' and 'C' Companies in an attack which put 12 German machine gun teams out of action, advanced the line by some 300 yards and resulted in the capture of over 200 prisoners.

Captain Nicholson was subsequently awarded the Military Cross for his conduct on 24 August, the official citation reading:

> 'For conspicuous gallantry and devotion to duty on 24 August at La Boisselle in command of his Company which fought its way to its objective in spite of very heavy machine gun and rifle fire. He held the position throughout the day, walking about in full view of the enemy, encouraging and reorganising the men. Later in the day, in conjunction with another Company, he attacked a crater and captured 200 prisoners.'

Second Lieutenant Blackburn was also awarded the Military Cross for his gallantry but was subsequently killed in action before he could receive it.

The exploits of two NCO's on this day attracted the attention of 18th Division's historian. Lance-Sergeant George William Hutchins rushed a German machine gunner with his bayonet during the initial advance and later led out a patrol to establish contact with a neighbouring battalion. He was severely wounded during the evening attack . Lance-Corporal Albert Walter Underwood volunteered to take up water to outpost positions. He did this four times, passing through heavy rifle and machine gun fire, and thus enabled his comrades to hold out through a long day.

Lance-Sergeant Hutchins, together with Sergeant J J Hurst and Private W Griffiths, was subsequently awarded the Distinguished Conduct Medal for conspicuous gallantry and devotion to duty displayed in this action.

The Battalion War Diary puts on record 'the tenacity of purpose of the troops engaged and the vigorous and forceful manner in which the attack was pressed to its goal.' Whilst acknowledging that the action was 'of a minor nature', the diarist points out that it was extremely important because, had it not been successful, the line could not have been advanced in subsequent attacks. A message of congratulation from Lieutenant-General Sir A J Godley, commanding III Corps, confirmed this statement.

Officer casualties on 24 August were:

Killed

2nd Lt R C Guy

Wounded

Lt C J M Marsh; 2nd Lt P W Rousell

5th Battalion at Carnoy

From Méaulte and La Boisselle the advance of both 12th and 18th Divisions continued rapidly eastwards, and by 26 August the 5th Royal Berkshires found themselves facing the village of Carnoy. Their orders on that day were to prepare for an attack between 4.00am and 4.30am. They marched up to the line by compass bearing and only reached their forming-up position at 4.45am, thus losing their barrage which was now falling some 1,500 yards ahead of them.

Their attack was made on both sides of the village and was met with heavy artillery and machine gun fire which caused a large number of casualties. The survivors managed to reach a spur which was their first objective and the leading troops were able then to fight their way to German trenches on a forward slope beyond the village facing the strip of woodland called Talus Boisé, west of Maricourt. A line was established late in the afternoon. On the following day the battalion moved forward and took up a position beyond Talus Boisé with its right on the small copse immediately to the east known as Machine Gun Wood. From here they moved back into Carnoy which had been meanwhile secured by other units and stayed there until the end of the month.

Second Lieutenant E W N Ellis was subsequently awarded the Military Cross for gallantry displayed during the attack as well as for his leadership of a company in the earlier capture of Méaulte. A similar award for gallant conduct in the two actions was made to Lieutenant B W Hougham.

Casualties for 26 August were reported as:

Officers killed

2nd Lts F J Tutton (died of wounds), W H Stapleton

Officers wounded

2nd Lt G W W Page

Other ranks

43 killed, 97 wounded, 31 missing

The Medical Officer, Captain W M Lansdale, had been killed by a shell the previous evening.

On 27 August the 5th Battalion moved forward and took over a position due east of Carnoy. From here they then moved back into the village which had in the meantime been secured by other units in the division and stayed there until the end of the month.

This day or two of comparative quiet for the men of the 5th Battalion contrasted sharply with the violence of the fighting in which the 8th Battalion were engaged on 27 August, described by the historian of the 18th Division as 'a day marked by prolonged and bitter struggle'.

8th Battalion at Trônes Wood

18th Division's advance had by 26 August taken 53rd Brigade to a position east of Montauban, facing Bernafay and Trônes Woods. The 8th Battalion, now under the command of Lieutenant-Colonel T M Banks DSO MC, was given as the objective for an attack on the following day the eastern edge of Trônes Wood. They were to form up on the line of the Bazentin-le-Grand to Montauban road with the 7th Royal West Kents on their right. Their advance, under a barrage, was planned to take them due eastwards to the eastern edge of Trônes Wood when they would then turn and clear the wood from the north. The operation was planned on the assumption that Delville Wood and Longueval were in the hands of 38th Division, thus providing a secure left flank.

This assumption was later found to be incorrect.

By 3.30am on 27 August the assembly on the forming-up position was complete and an hour later the leading lines moved forward to catch the barrage which was timed to open at 4.55am. Enemy machine gun fire was encountered, especially from the left where the flank of the

Trônes Wood (IWM Q4882)

attack had been exposed through the absence of 38th Division, temporarily driven out of Longueval. On the right, enemy posts were cleared without appreciable loss.

The second line of enemy resistance came on the Bernafay-Longueval road. This again was negotiated with success on the right whilst the left companies were held up by flank fire. The right pushed on and took prisoners between the Longueval road and Trônes Wood. The leading right company, 'D', now considerably weakened, succeeded in getting into the wood but came under fire from Waterlot Farm to the east. 'B' Company had meanwhile carried out their right turn and formed up in the middle of the wood astride a light railway, facing south.

The situation was now quite critical, with 'A' and 'C' Companies held well back on the left and large numbers of the enemy advancing from Waterlot Farm. Longueval and Delville Wood were also full of enemy troops. The German advance from Waterlot Farm was checked but at a cost, Second Lieutenant F W Hopwood commanding 'D' Company being killed here. It was found impossible to hold on to the eastern edge of Trônes Wood because of enfilade fire, but a stand in the trenches just to the west of the wood seemed feasible and Colonel Banks rallied the men for a withdrawal there.

Captain Wykes, Acting Second-in-Command of the battalion, volunteered to go back and try to bring up the left hand companies. This he succeeded in doing after half an hour, although incurring a number of casualties. Meanwhile 'B' Company had started its advance southwards through the wood but had to halt because of our own heavy shelling, and it too fell back to the trenches just west of the wood. At about 8.00am a counter attack by a battalion of the German 2nd Guards Division pushed through the southern portion of the wood and menaced the whole of the Royal Berkshires' position. But they were held and their gains were limited. The remainder of the day was spent in reorganisation and replenishment of ammunition in preparation for a counter attack.

At 6.30pm an intense bombardment was opened on the southern part of Trônes Wood. After half an hour 'B' Company together with two companies from the 10th Essex moved out under the barrage and took the enemy by surprise. In the hand-to-hand fighting which followed, three German officers and 70 other ranks were taken prisoner, about 50 were killed and 20 machine guns captured. Posts were then organised and consolidated at the eastern edge of the wood. The Germans also maintained posts in the northern part of the wood and on the ground to the east but these, in the words of the battalion diarist, 'were rendered largely innocuous by the command of the ground captured and the night passed quietly without enemy reaction'.

A German perspective on this counter-attack is given by the historian of the 2nd Guards Grenadier Regiment writing in 1929:

'At 7.00pm a heavy bombardment opened and lasted for forty-five minutes. Then attacks came from the north and the west. Three of our companies held the western edge of Trônes Wood, the fourth on the extreme right was surrounded and in spite of fierce resistance was cut down. Now the enemy attacked two of the remaining companies from the rear. After severe and costly fighting we had to abandon the wood. Only one company was able to retire in some order to the south-eastern corner. About 40 men from the rest of the battalion helped to form a defensive post here from which they were able to hold up any further enemy advance.'

For conspicuous gallantry displayed in the day's actions Captain Wykes was awarded a Bar to his Military Cross won at Ovillers in 1916. In the words of the official citation:

'He controlled the direction of the battalion under heavy machine gun fire and when the Company ran into our halted barrage, he showed great coolness. By his leadership the resistance of the enemy was finally overcome and he was wounded himself whilst disposing of one of the enemy who had shot an officer.'

Sergeant S Bagnall was awarded the Distinguished Conduct Medal for gallantry displayed in the prompt action he took when his company was held up by a German machine gun. He dashed at the gun and captured it, despite being severely wounded whilst doing so.

At midnight the 8th Royal Berkshires were relieved and moved back to Caterpillar Valley. From there they went into reserve near Guillemont.

Officer casualties in the action were recorded as:

Killed

2nd Lts S M Brown, G W Buckley, F W Hopwood

Wounded

Capt W Rogerson (RAMC); 2nd Lts J Buck, J Davies, H Martin

Total other ranks casualties for the actions on 8, 24 and 27 August were:
    79 killed, 225 wounded, 8 wounded and missing, 10 missing

8 Attacks at St Pierre Vaast Wood

The two Royal Berkshire battalions were once again to be in action together in mid-September, when the advance of Fourth Army had taken it to the outer defences of the Hindenburg Line. Here 12th and 18th Divisions would be neighbours in the line.

In the meantime, units of 18th Division, including the 8th Royal Berkshires, fought a series of actions on the northern sector of Fourth Army's front. To the south, the Australians were winning their celebrated victories at Péronne and Mont St Quentin.

On 1 September the 8th Battalion moved up to positions near the village of Combles. On their right, units of 47th Division had been ordered to take Rancourt and to advance as far as the south-east corner of St Pierre Vaast Wood. The Royal Berkshires were to attack the central part of the wood, with the higher ground in the wood to the north being allocated to the 10th Essex. On their left the 7th Royal West Kents faced the village of Saillisel. Once in the wood, the 8th Battalion were to form a defensive flank facing south.

The assembly on the western edge of the wood was completed by 3.30am on 2 September. The barrage opened up at 5.30am, moved forward 20 minutes later, and, with the troops following close behind its protecting cover, all objectives had been secured by 7.10am. The Royal

Area of the 8th Battalion's actions at St Pierre Vaast Wood

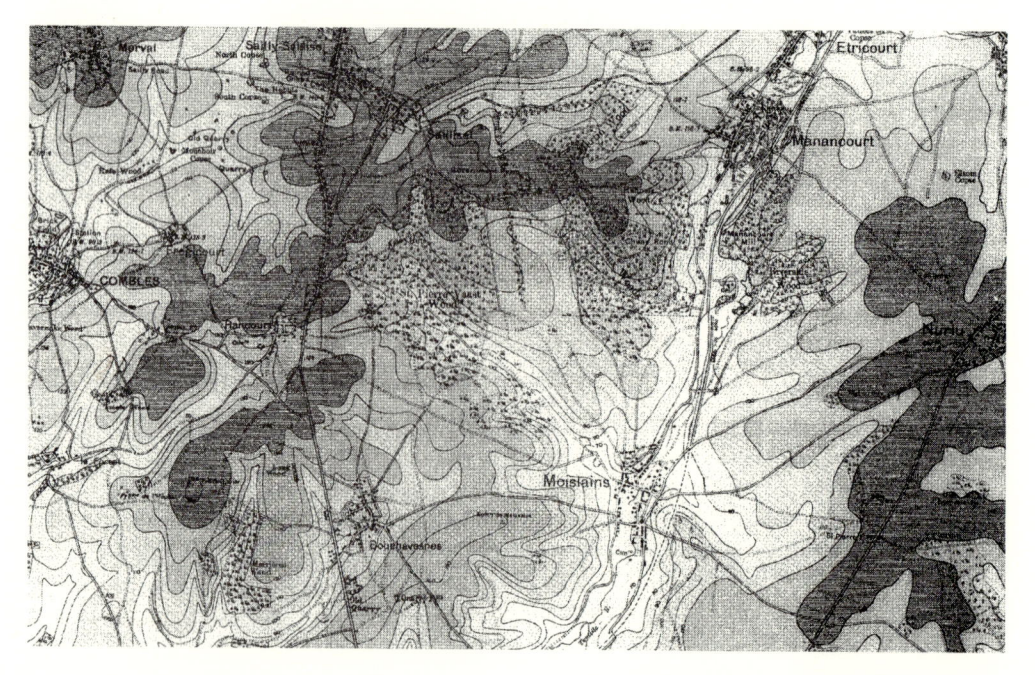

Berkshires suffered no casualties and took over 100 prisoners, including three officers. Heavy German shell fire then started at 10.30am and continued for the rest of the day, causing a number of casualties.

The historian of 18th Division analysed this action in terms of the progress which was being made in tactics:

'The taking of St Pierre Vaast Wood was another example of the methods adopted by General Lee (General Officer Commanding 18th Division) during the period 22 August to 5 September that marked the transition from trench to open warfare. It was an instance of capturing an important position by refusing it, by taking it in side and rear. The 10th Essex and the 7th Royal West Kents secured the dominating ground on the fringes of the wood, after which the wood itself was cleared by two companies of the Berkshires who suffered no casualties in the process. All the casualties that occurred in St Pierre Vaast Wood came from hostile shelling when the wood was in our hands.'

At 4.00am on 3 September 'C' Company of the Royal Berkshires sent out patrols to a trench situated between St Pierre Vaast Wood and Vaux Wood to the east. They reported it to be unoccupied. The 10th Essex were then ordered forward and took the high ground overlooking the village of Manancourt to the north-east and the Canal du Nord. In order to support them, the 8th Battalion moved 'C' and 'D' Companies through to the eastern edge of Hennois Wood, itself an extension of Vaux Wood. Here they were met with heavy machine gun and artillery fire which frustrated any attempts to establish a line facing the canal.

At 5.00pm the two remaining companies, 'A' and 'B', were ordered up from reserve. 'A' reached the canal by 8.30pm and 'B' sent out patrols to secure a passage of the Tortille River which flows east of the canal through Manancourt. They managed to cross the canal but had to withdraw in face of heavy enemy fire.

On 4 September at 8.00am patrols again moved forward and on the right secured a footing on the slopes above the Tortille. By 8.00pm they had reached the edge of the next wood to the east, Riverside Wood, which overlooks the village of Nurlu, soon to become familiar to the men of the 5th Battalion. The Germans were thus forced to retire from their advanced posts here. In these actions, Second Lieutenant Grant distinguished himself by rushing a German post and killing its garrison.

Before they were relieved by units of 12th Division, the 8th Battalion made good their line on the eastern edge of Riverside Wood. During the relief, 'C' Company suffered badly through gas casualties.

On 5 September at 9.30am the men moved into bivouacs near Montauban and started a period of training and reorganisation.

On that same day a German shell exploded on Méricourt station, between Amiens and Albert, killing or wounding 56 men of a draft of 176 reinforcements who were on their way to join the 8th Battalion. Of the 32 men who were killed or who died of their wounds, at least half were only 18 years of age and were presumably coming up to the line for the first time. One local communal cemetery, at Méricourt l'Abbé, contains 21 of their headstones.

The headstones in Méricourt l'Abbé Communal Cemetery of the 21 men coming up as reinforcements for the 8th Battalion

Officer casualties in the actions at the woods were:
Wounded (on 3 September)

2nd Lts W G Davies, A E Logsdon

Gassed (on 4 September)

2nd Lts E W Clark, T C Halliburton

On 7 September Major-General R P Lee received on behalf of 18th Division a message from the General Officer Commanding III Corps, Lieutenant-General Sir A J Godley, which included a summary of the achievements of the division since the beginning of the Allied offensive:

'I wish to congratulate and thank all ranks under your command for the very fine work which has been done by the Division since it went into the line practically a month ago. For the greater part of this month the Division has been fighting daily and incessantly, and has to its credit the crossing of the Ancre and the Canal du Nord and the making of bridges over them, the capture of Albert, Tara and Usna Hills, the craters at La Boisselle, Montauban, Bernafay, Trônes and Leuze Woods, Combles, Frégicourt, Saillisel, St Pierre Vaast Wood, Vaux Wood and the whole of the country as far east as the Canal du Nord, a distance of seventeen miles.'

With many of these names, above all perhaps with La Boisselle and Trônes Wood, the men of the 8th Royal Berkshires had forged their own associations. The concluding sentence of Lieutenant-General Godley's message applied in full measure to them:

'You may well be proud of the valour and endurance which the Division has daily and incessantly displayed in order to enable it to add such a record to its long list of notable achievements.'

9 Towards the Hindenburg Line

The Fourth Army actions fought from 18 to 24 September were designed to establish a footing in the outer defences of the Hindenburg Line, the last major German defensive system. Fourth Army's III Corps was to operate on a 7,000 yard front in the northern sector. On their right was the Australian Corps.

12th and 18th Divisions with respectively the 5th and the 8th Royal Berkshires formed the centre of III Corps' attack. They had the task between them of capturing the fortified villages of Epéhy, Ronssoy, Basse Boulogne and Lempire, together with a number of the posts or strongpoints which were a feature of the outer defences of the Hindenburg Line.

The 5th Royal Berkshires had earlier in the month been one of the units relieving 18th Division troops following the latter's advance to the Canal du Nord and Riverside Wood. They had then initially been in reserve for 12th Division's subsequent attack on the village of Nurlu. On 5 September they had taken part in the third, and finally successful, attempt to clear the village despite continuing strong German resistance.

Casualties in this action were reported as:

Officers killed

Capt B W Hougham

Officers wounded

2nd Lt P P Ralph

Other ranks

12 wounded

From 8 September the 5th Battalion had been out of the line at Nurlu, rehearsing for the forthcoming major assault on the Hindenburg Line. The 8th Battalion had also had a respite following their success at St Pierre Vaast Wood. They had been with 18th Division near Montauban, also in training.

The Fourth Army plan for the attack on 18 September placed 12th Division on the left of 18th. Their main objective was the village of Epéhy, whilst 18th Division were allotted Ronssoy, Basse Boulogne and Lempire. A problem for the troops of both divisions was the 'basin', a strongly defended position in the triangle formed by Ronssoy, Epéhy and St Émilie, the village from which 18th Division would start their attack. To avoid a frontal assault on this feature, 18th Division were to attack south of the spur running from Ronssoy to St Émilie whilst 12th Division attacked west of the spur from Epéhy to St Émilie. Having captured Ronssoy and Epéhy the two divisions were to wheel inwards and roll up the German main line of defence which ran between the two.

8th Battalion at Lempire

Of the two Royal Berkshire battalions, the 8th were the first to move up to the line. They, together with the other units in 53rd Brigade, took over trenches east of St Émilie on the night of 16/17 September and carried out patrols. A daylight patrol on 17 September brought in four prisoners from the 2nd Guards Regiment, a German unit so far not identified as being in the opposing trenches.

The attack, which started in wet weather and poor visibility at 5.20am on 18 September, was led on the 18th Division front by the 7th Royal West Kents. There was no preliminary bombardment, the infantry with the support of three of the four tanks allocated to the division, moved forward under a creeping barrage on to their first objective. After an hour here, sheltered by a protective barrage, they moved on towards their second objective. German resistance was strong and the

The 18th Division's attack front 18–24 September 1918

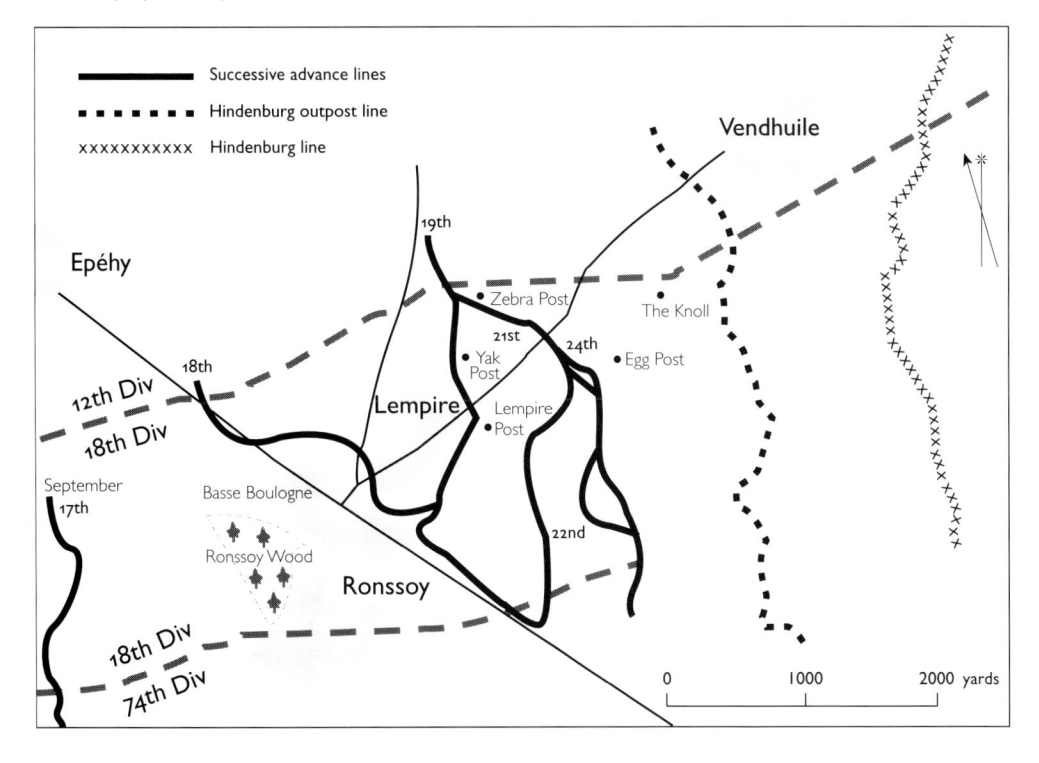

Towards the Hindenburg Line 47

terrain was difficult. Much of the fighting took place in the complicated trench system of former British lines, fiercely defended now by German machine gunners and small groups of infantry. The second objectives in this sector were not taken.

The results of the first day's fighting, in which the 8th Royal Berkshires took no direct part, were the capture of Ronssoy and Basse Boulogne and of a number of posts.

The 8th Battalion's main engagement came on the next day. At 8.30am they reached their assembly posts and at 11.00am they attacked under a creeping barrage with the object of clearing the Germans from the northern part of the village of Lempire and establishing a line facing east and linking a number of posts which bore the names of Lempire, Yak and Zebra. The troops encountered stiff resistance with heavy machine gun fire coming from the village and from three small copses on their right. However they reached their objectives, an achievement which the historian of 18th Division acknowledged:

> 'They (the Berkshires) had marched forward under cover of the contours of the ground, only to find themselves, as at Trônes Wood, pushing a wedge into the Germans with their flanks exposed. Two posts on their right were as yet untaken, and a raking fire from these points tore their right flank to pieces. But on their left they were screened by a high bank north of Lempire, and the company on that side went straight up the road, got through in a brisk and dashing manner, and caused the Germans to retire hurriedly. In fact, the Berkshires came on so quickly that they captured an unopened mail bag.'

Two NCOs distinguished themselves in this action. Lance-Corporal James Cecil Masters reorganised a bombing party in the face of heavy machine gunfire, bombed up a trench towards the guns and, on reaching the German post, captured two machine guns and took nine prisoners. Lance-Corporal Arthur James Rawlings, who was in charge of a company of stretcher bearers, took them repeatedly into the open and brought back wounded men under heavy fire. When three bearers had been hit whilst trying to bring in a badly wounded officer, Lance-Corporal Rawlings went out, dressed the officer's wounds and brought him back safely.

Seen from the German side, according to the historian of the 1st Guard Grenadier Regiment writing in 1932, the attack started in the following way:

> 'The night (of 18/19 September) passed relatively quietly but before daybreak an enemy bombardment opened on both our neighbouring positions. Our front was still quiet but we all knew it was the calm before the storm. As it grew lighter numerous enemy aircraft

appeared and from 9.30am onwards we could make out groups of British infantry in front and to our right. Immediately we put down a heavy bombardment but the enemy had a counter: he released smoke and made artillery observation impossible. Soon afterwards machine gun and rifle fire announced the start of the attack on one of our companies.'

The German historian then quotes from the personal account of a Lieutenant Schröder which refers to positions north of Lempire where the 8th Royal Berkshires attacked:

'The enemy following up his barrage emerged from the ruined houses in the village and got into our company's trenches after working his way up a sunken road. Two of our machine guns which were defending the road were destroyed by enemy artillery. Since our company was in danger of being cut off we fought our way back to the communication trench and reached our defensive post.'

What followed the 8th Battalion's action on 19 September is disputed in the records. The Battalion War Diary mentions no fighting for the remainder of the month, whereas the historian of 18th Division has them involved two days later on 21 September, when part of the divisional objective was The Knoll, a prominent feature giving observation over the whole of the section of the Hindenburg Line facing the divisional front. 53rd Brigade were allotted seven tanks to help them, with the 10th Essex having the main responsibility for taking The Knoll itself. The Essex battalion managed to make some progress but were held up by heavy machine gun fire and suffered severe casualties, losing by evening 280 men. According to the 53rd Brigade War Diary, the 8th Battalion was holding the line for this operation.

At this point, according to the historian of 18th Division, the 10th Essex were relieved by the 8th Royal Berkshires who at 12.15am on the following day were called upon to make a bombing attack on the German posts south of The Knoll known as Egg and Fleeceall. Once again heavy resistance was encountered and the battalion was unable to take its objectives. This account is supported by the 53rd Brigade War Diary.

What is not in dispute is that Egg Post had to be left untaken when 18th Division came out of the line on the night of 24/25 September. The 8th Battalion went back with the division to Combles for rest, the 2nd American Corps taking over their positions.

Casualties for the month of September were reported as:

Officers killed

2nd Lt R Cumbley

Headstone of Second Lieutenant R Cumbley in Unicorn Cemetery, Lempire

Officers died of wounds

2nd Lt A J Preston

Officers wounded

2nd Lts E W Clarke, W G Davies, T C Halliburton, A E Logsdon, A J Preston, E J H Sonnex

Other ranks

44 killed, 1 died of wounds, 145 wounded, 55 gassed, 12 missing

The Fourth Army Commander, General Rawlinson, sent a message on 24 September to III Corps Commander in which he reviewed the record of the four divisions in the Corps since the opening of the Allied offensive at the begining of August:

'The 12th, 18th and 58th Divisions have been fighting continuously since 6th August, while the 74th Division has had heavy fighting during the last three weeks. Although opposed to the Alpine Corps and four of the finest German Divisions, two of which have reinforced the line within the last forty-eight hours, they have by determination and hard fighting gained ground which is of the utmost importance, and which German maps show to be part of the main Hindenburg defences, and were to be held at all costs.'

5th Battalion at Epéhy

The 5th Battalion, unlike the 8th, did take part in the first day's actions on 18 September, although not in the initial assault. 12th Division's attack at Epéhy on that day was led by 36th and 35th Brigades whilst the Royal Berkshires were in support with 37th Brigade near the village of Guyencourt. German resistance in this sector too was fierce and by late afternoon their troops were still holding out at the northern end of Epéhy. Casualties in 35th Brigade had been very high and three companies of the 5th Royal Berkshires were brought in as reinforcements. Their first task was to help clear the village and, when this was accomplished, to secure trenches near Tétard Wood on its eastern outskirts. The battalion's performance here earned them recognition from the historian of Fourth Army: 'The 5th Royal Berkshire did especially good work and was fighting for most of the night.'

At midnight on 21/22 September the battalion went into action again to capture the section of the German line running through a strong point at Little Priel Farm, some 4,000 yards due east of Epéhy. Weather conditions were favourable and by 2.00am they had taken all objectives.

Battle of Epéhy. Three soldiers resting on ground near Epéhy captured by the 12th Division on that day. 18 September 1918 (IWM Q11326)

They were heavily shelled in these positions for most of the next day. The historian of 12th Division recorded their attack:

'In excellent spirits and full of determination, the Berkshires made a brilliant bayonet charge, resulting in heavy fighting in and around Heythorp Post and Heythorp Trench. All resistance was overcome and within an hour Little Priel Farm was captured. One officer and and eighteen men were taken prisoner, fifty dead counted about the position, and forty machine guns found in the ruins of the farm. In fact, to describe it as a post "bristling" with machine guns would be no exaggeration.'

The battalion's last engagement on this part of the front came two days later on 24 September when the so-called Dados Loop position was the objective. This German strong point to the north of Little Priel Farm was situated on the crest of a spur leading down to the Escaut River and commanded all-round views. During the afternoon of 24 September the 9th Royal Fusiliers made a number of attempts to take the position but without success. A further attempt at 10.00pm by 'A' Company of the 5th Royal Berkshires also failed. They were still trying to take the position two days later and it was not until 30 September, during the

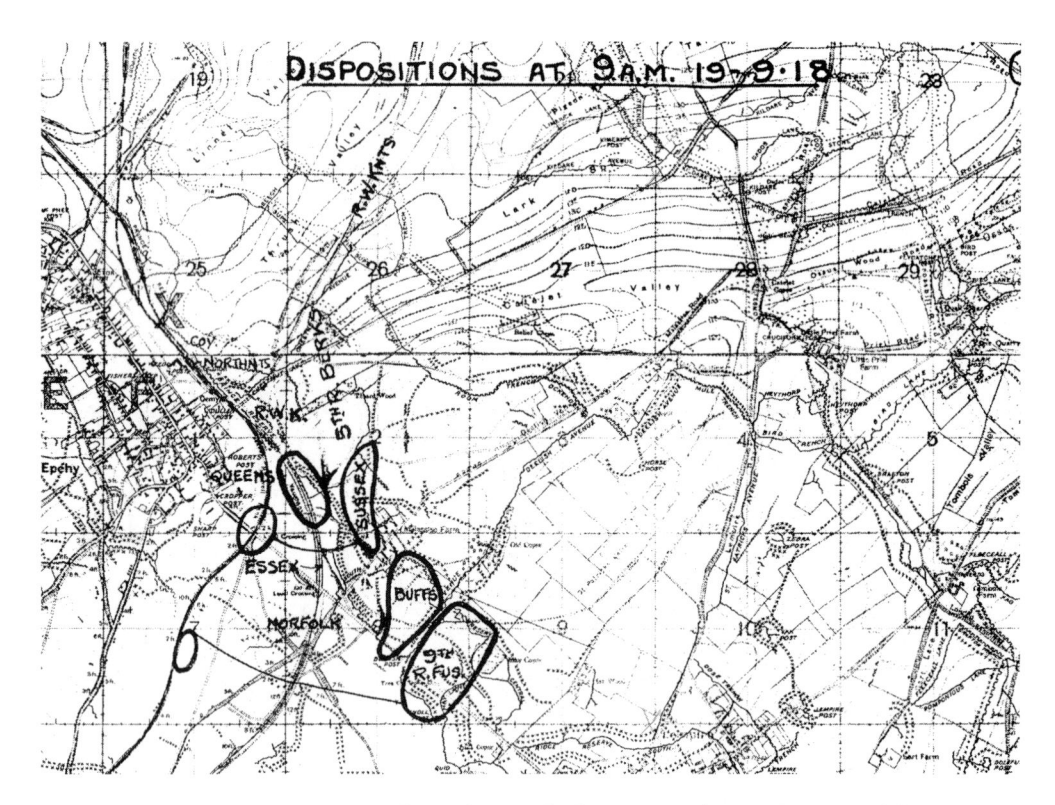

The 5th Battalion's positions at Tétard Wood on 19 September 1918 (PRO WO95/1827)

main assault on the Hindenburg Line, that Dados Loop fell.

At this time the role of 12th Division was to protect the flank of the attack being made on their right by the 27th Division of the United States Army. The 12th Division was relieved on 29/30 September by which time it had been in action for twelve consecutive days and was so reduced in numbers that it needed reinforcing before it would be fit again for active operations. The 5th Battalion moved back to Guyencourt on 30 September.

Casualties for the period 18-30 September were reported as:

Officers killed

2nd Lt E F Bond

Officers wounded

2nd Lts W A Buckingham, T C Enever, F S Hawkins, A V Saunders, D M Thompson

Other ranks

250 killed, wounded or missing

Whilst the main assault on the Hindenburg Line was still in progress, 12th Division was taken out of Fourth Army and moved north to First Army's front, joining VIII Corps operating in the Vimy sector. The link

Their Duty Done

between the two 'Royal Berkshire' divisions was thus broken and they were to fight the war to a conclusion on different sectors of the front.

12th Division and the 5th Royal Berkshires could now look back on a 26-mile advance since the Battle of Amiens on 8 August which had taken them from Morlancourt to the St Quentin Canal. General Rawlinson's personal farewell message to 12th Division, dated 2 October 1918, contained the following tribute:

'A long list of successes, including Morlancourt, Carnoy, Hardecourt, Maurepas and Nurlu, culminating in the capture of the strongly-fortified village of Epéhy, constitutes a record which has seldom been equalled, and I wish to convey to every officer, NCO and man of the 12th Division my gratitude for the magnificent example they have set, and my warmest thanks for the invaluable service they have rendered.'

10 The last weeks: 5th Battalion

After leaving Fourth Army and moving with 12th Division to the north, the 5th Royal Berkshires quickly neared the end of their active service. Although there was still some hard fighting to be done, the battalion's progress eastwards in pursuit of a retreating German army was achieved without the kind of losses suffered in the earlier weeks of the campaign.

On 5 October the battalion arrived on First Army's front in the sector south of Lens. Within a few days of their arrival, signs of a German withdrawal became apparent. In striking contrast to the stiff resistance offered on the approach to the main Hindenburg Line defences further south, the defenders of the Drocourt-Quéant Line (the Wotan Stellung) put up little fight. This position, constructed in 1917 as the northern extension of the Hindenburg Line and running some four miles east of Lens, was taken on 11 October. The 5th Battalion War Diary for that day recorded laconically:

> 'The advance continued unopposed, in conjunction with the 9th Royal Fusiliers on the right, to the Drocourt-Quéant Line which was occupied at 5.00pm.'

One disadvantage of this return to open warfare was noted by the

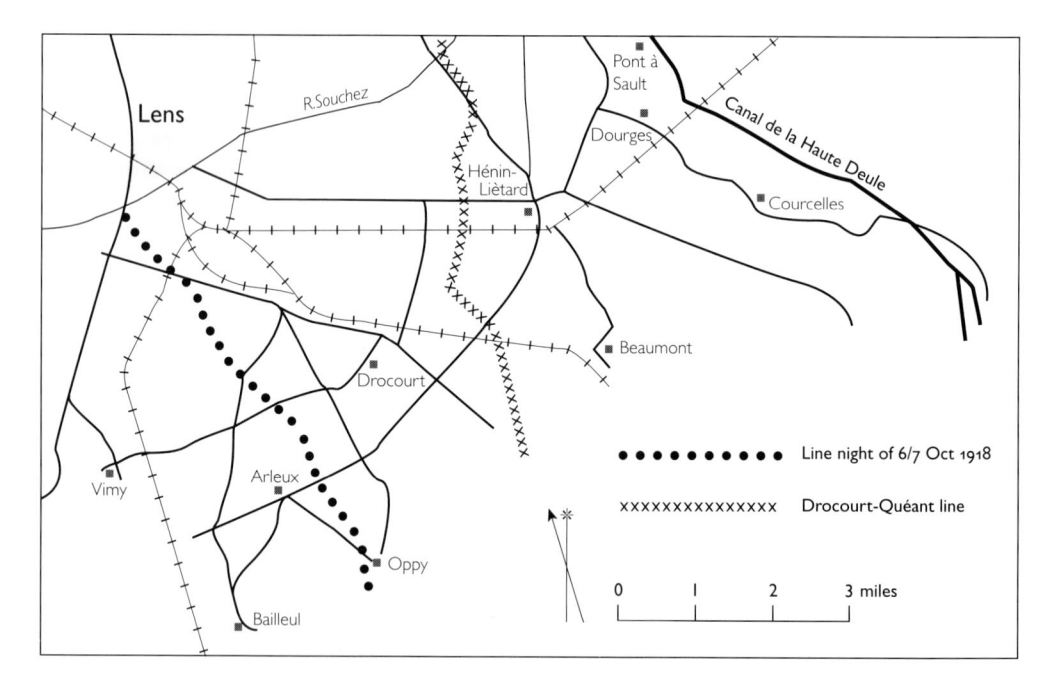

Area of the 5th Battalion's actions in October 1918

54   *Their Duty Done*

historian of the 12th Division. Because of the rapidity of the movements, communication by telephone became impossible – lines could not be erected quickly enough – and the men had to rely on visual signalling.

The last serious opposition encountered came some days later, when units of 12th Division were approaching the obstacle of the Haute Deule Canal. Lieutenant-Colonel E H J Nicholls had just taken over command of the 5th Battalion again and the village of Dourges, west of the canal, was taken on 13 October despite strong opposition. Patrols then reported that the Germans were holding the east bank of the canal in some force and that all bridges had been blown.

Although the Battalion War Diary entry for 15 October mentioned only reduced enemy shell fire and stated that a further advance was impossible, at least one act of bravery by a member of the battalion took place on that day – and was recognised.

Second Lieutenant John Edgell Rickword, who had joined the battalion in September 1917 and had twice been wounded since then, volunteered to cross the canal and undertake a reconnaisance. After making the crossing, he was spotted by the enemy who covered him with their machine guns. Despite this, he worked his way along the eastern bank of the canal and brought back valuable information. For his gallantry he was awarded the Military Cross.

On the following day patrols reported that the east bank of the canal was clear and 'B' Company freed a passage at Pont à Sault to the north. A line was then established on the east bank and a pontoon bridge erected. The three days here cost the battalion the heaviest casualties of the whole month: nine killed, forty wounded and three missing.

The advance thereafter was characterised by a novel experience, that of finding the villages still occupied by their inhabitants. As the historian of the 12th Division observed:

> 'The presence of the French in the villages showed that the retreat of the Germans was now something more than a withdrawal. Previous demolitions had been systematic, and civilians had been compelled to evacuate their homes as the enemy retired. Now there was evidently no time for this, undamaged villages were found by our troops, and the enthusiasm of the inhabitants, after four years of enemy occupation, can be better imagined than described.'

What turned out to be the final action of the war for the 5th Royal Berkshires came on 28 October when an attempt was being made to establish a bridgehead over the Canal de l'Escaut. There was strong German opposition here, with heavy shelling, and Captain C A Mallam, who had been battalion adjutant for three years, was severely

Second Lieutenant JE Rickword

Captain C A Mallam

The last weeks: 5th Battalion

wounded. He died of his wounds on the following day.

Two days later the men of the 5th Battalion settled into billets in the village of Flines. Their war was over.

Captain C A Mallam's original grave marker. He is buried in Douai British Cemetery

11 The last weeks: 8th Battalion

The last weeks of the war meant for the 8th Battalion a continuation of their hard-fought campaigning virtually to the end, with three separate attacks made within a fortnight against what the 18th Division historian described as: 'an enemy on the defensive, desperate, in fair strength, and still greatly skilled in military cunning.'

On 2 October the battalion was transported by bus to Allonville, where the men went into billets with the other units of 53rd Brigade. Here they stayed for two weeks during which time the Battalion War Diary recorded sadly that on 12 October the battalion football team under Captain G W H Nicholson had lost to the 10th Essex 2:4. On 14 October however – under Corporal W H Goodey – they beat the 7th Royal West Kents 4:3. Perhaps in revenge, Captain C Tuff, attached to the battalion from the West Kents, gave the men on that same day a lecture on Baghdad.

The countryside in which they were now campaigning, east of Le Cateau and the River Selle, was compared by the historian of Fourth Army with the open, rolling terrain covered since the crossing of the St Quentin Canal:

> 'East of the Selle the slopes became more abrupt, small streams ran in the valleys, and there were large tracts of woodland. The pasture land between these tracts was cut up into innumerable small enclosures bounded by high, thick hedges, which, while constituting a serious obstacle to an infantry advance, at the same time afforded it excellent cover from view, except at short ranges. L'Évêque Wood, covering an area of some four square miles, had been cleared of standing timber over three parts of its area, and the cleared spaces were covered with brambles and undergrowth. Apart from the difficulty of maintaining touch and direction, the passage of this wood did not present any serious obstacle, except by night or in a fog.'

Attack at L'Évêque Wood

On 22 October the 8th Battalion moved to Le Cateau for 18th Division's attack on the following day. The larger canvas of operations was the plan of Third and Fourth Armies to gain the western edge of the Forest of Mormal in continuation of the general advance.

By late evening the men were in their assembly positions east of the village facing L'Évêque Wood. The ground over which the attack was

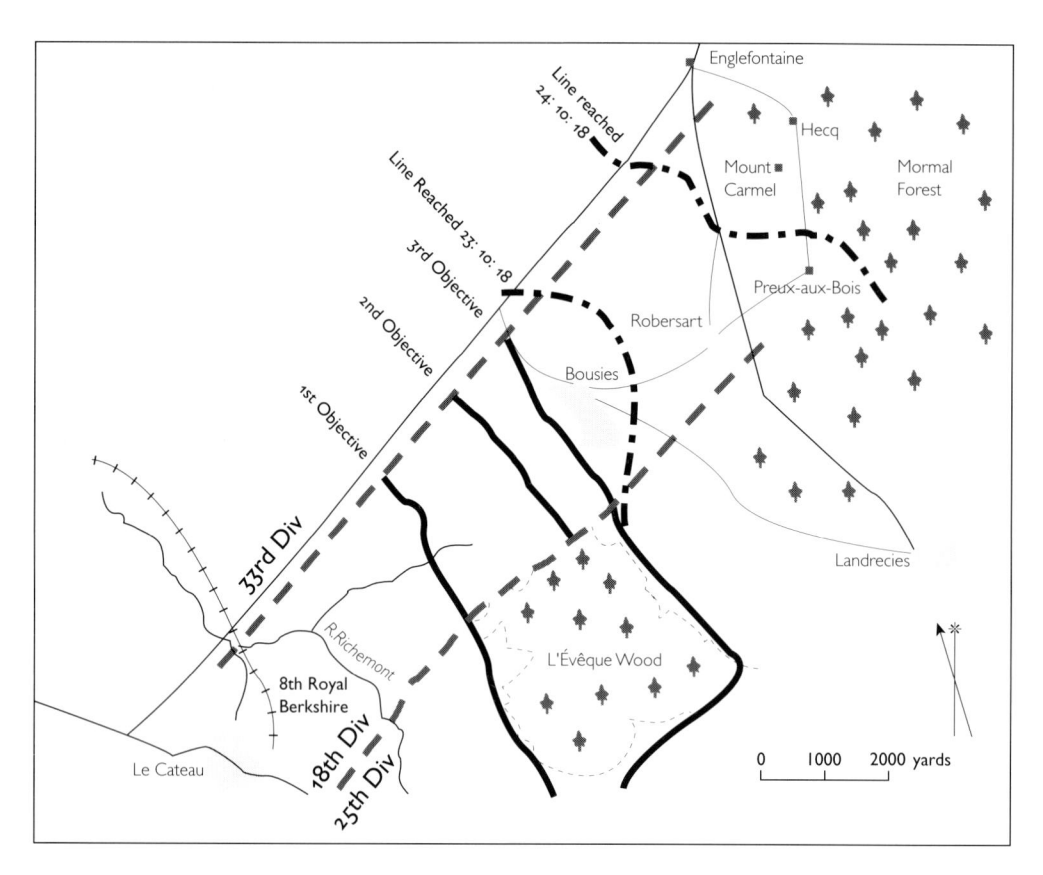

The 18th Division's attack front 23–24 October 1918

to be made was rough grassland with no connected trench systems but with strong German defensive positions organised in depth around machine gun posts. Some 1,000 yards from the British line the ground shelved to the Richemont River, itself only a shallow stream, and rose more steeply on the other side to a plateau where old practice trenches gave the Germans some prepared positions.

Zero hour was 1.20am on 23 October. The Royal Berkshires' assembly point was a deep railway cutting east of Le Cateau from where they would advance onto the second objective. Enemy shelling here caused 15 casualties, including Captain W H Ferguson RAMC. Despite a leg wound Captain Ferguson continued to attend to the casualties, helping to extricate men from a temporary dressing station which was blown in by a gas shell. He was then wounded for a second time, severely enough to be sent back to England six days later. For his gallantry and devotion to duty he was awarded a Bar to his Military Cross won earlier in the year for carrying wounded men to safety through a heavy barrage.

At 1.15am the companies moved out of the cutting with 'D' on the right, 'C' in the centre, 'B' on the left and 'A' in support. A creeping bar-

Their Duty Done

rage moving forward at the rate of 25 yards a minute supported the attack. At 2.20am they 'leap-frogged' through the 10th Essex and the 7th Royal West Kents on their way to the second objective. The first opposition they met was at Richemont River which had already proved a serious obstacle for the brigade. It was wider than it had appeared to be from aerial photographs, and to compound the problems the four tanks allotted to the brigade had been knocked out of action. When 'B' Company of the battalion reached the river they were held up by a machine gun nest missed by the 10th Essex. Second Lieutenant J Grant was killed here and most of company headquarters became casualties.

Arriving near the original first objective, a line running from the western corner of L'Évêque Wood, they found the 10th Essex held up in a sunken road. No progress could be made until 54th Brigade and its tanks came up on their left flank. At daybreak the enemy began to retire and Captain M Wykes took the leading companies of the two battalions and rushed the road, capturing over 30 light and heavy machine guns. The advance then continued and the second objective, a line some 1,500 yards beyond the first and running from the northern corner of the wood, was taken by 8.30am and held throughout the day.

Continuing rivalry between the Royal Berkshires and the Royal West Kents is hinted at in an anecdote recorded by the historian of 18th Division. During the day's fighting the West Kents apparently came across a disused French threshing machine and chalked on it in large letters: 'Captured by the 8th Royal Berks.'

The results of a day's hard fighting, as far as 18th Division as a whole was concerned, were considered to be extremely satisfactory with the final objectives all being secured and a total advance made of some 8,000 yards.

Casualties in this action were reported as

Officers killed

2nd Lts N H G Blackburn, J Grant

Officers wounded

Capt W H Ferguson (RAMC);
2nd Lts F W Beeny, W Deans, W A McConnell

Other ranks

19 killed, 1 died of wounds, 67 wounded, 3 missing

Attack on Mount Carmel

On the following day orders were received for 53rd Brigade to cooperate with 33rd Division in a forthcoming attack on Mount Carmel, just to the west of the Forest of Mormal. Mount Carmel, some 1,200 yards from the British line, was in fact no more than an undulating field slightly higher than the surrounding countryside. The Germans held the eastern edge of the field with a line of posts on the road connecting the villages of Hecq and Preux-aux-Bois. For the attack the 10th Essex were on the right, the 8th Royal Berkshires and two companies of the 7th Royal West Kents on the left.

At midnight on 25/26 October the men moved to their assembly positions and the advance began at 1.00am. Enemy machine gun fire made progress slow and strong opposition was encountered on the road from Englefontaine to Robersart, to the west of Mount Carmel. Here the right of the attack was held up, although the left continued to make progress. By 1.40am two platoons of 'B' Company had reached their objective, but heavy casualties caused at daybreak by enemy artillery and machine gun fire forced them to fall back to a sunken road immediately to the east of the Robersart road. The final line occupied and consolidated was 400 yards short of Mount Carmel but it was considered to be a more easily defensible position than the original objective. During the action Lieutenant-Colonel N B Hudson, who had resumed command of the battalion only two days earlier, was slightly wounded. Captain G W H Nicholson took his place temporarily.

The 53rd Brigade after-action report on this attack praises Lieutenant-Colonel Hudson's contribution:

> 'Lieutenant-Colonel N B Hudson MC rendered a most valuable assistance throughout the operation. It was in large measure due to his personal exertions and gallantry that a satisfactory line was established and held.'

The Forest of Mormal

At 9.00pm on 3 November, 53rd and 54th Brigades of 18th Division took up their assembly positions for what was to be their last action of the war. The objective for XIII Corps, to which 18th Division now belonged, was the southern portion of the Forest of Mormal. This attack would form part of a large-scale offensive by the First, Third and Fourth Armies to be delivered on a 30-mile front.

The historian of Fourth Army gave a picture of the forest at that time:

> 'Mormal Forest itself covers an area of forty square miles, but much of it had been cut down for timber by the enemy during his occupation, and there were, therefore, numerous clearings; in

those portions which were untouched by the axe the undergrowth was very dense and hampered movement. The whole forest offered great opportunities for resolute defence. Owing to its size, density, and good interior communications it was capable of sheltering considerable forces, whilst its large expanse made it difficult for artillery to deal with effectively.'

The 8th Royal Berkshires with the 10th Essex on their right were to pass through the 7th Royal West Kents and the 2nd Bedfords of 54th Brigade attacking from the line established at Mount Carmel. They formed up at 7.35am on 4 November. It is worth noting that at this time the battalion could muster only 15 officers and 243 other ranks.

Their objective was the 'red line' running north-south through the forest 3,000 yards distant. The West Kents in the first wave had met with considerable resistance and were held up at the village of Hecq. This delayed the advance of the Royal Berkshires, but two of their companies, 'C' and 'D', succeeded in pushing through on the northern edge of the attack front and 'C' reached the red line at about noon. Here, under the leadership of Lieutenant F J Powell, they maintained their position for over three hours although they were reduced to 36 men and both their flanks were exposed. In recognition of this achievement Lieutenant Powell was subsequently awarded the Military Cross.

The two companies on the left of the 10th Essex, 'A' and 'B', were unable to get to their forming-up positions as the area had not been completely cleared. 'A' Company under Captain T K Pickard needed three hours to fight its way to a second assembly point and then on to the red line by 3.00pm. This involved working round and rushing machine gun posts, an action which was well carried out, but still cost the company a number of casualties. 'B' Company was not involved in this fighting but had placed posts at the southern exits of the forest.

General Rawlinson's message to 18th Division of 4 November acknowledged the skill and the bravery demonstrated on that day:

'Please convey to 18th Division my congratulations on their success today in forcing their way through the Forest of Mormal. The precision with which the various columns advanced through the forest shows the staff work and leadership were thoroughly good, whilst the gallantry and determination of the troops is deserving of high praise.'

Casualties in this action were recorded as:

Officers killed

2nd Lt L J Field

Other ranks

10 killed, 2 died of wounds, 35 wounded, 1 missing

Front line action for the 8th Battalion thus ended in countryside familiar to the men of the original British Expeditionary Force who in August 1914 had marched down past the Forest of Mormal on their way from Mons. The battalion returned to Le Cateau where on 11 November news of the armistice was, according to the battalion diarist, received by the troops very quietly.

12 Disbandment

5th Battalion

The men of the 5th Royal Berkshires marked Armistice Day with a church parade. Full battalion strength at this time was 34 officers and 708 other ranks. By the beginning of the New Year demobilisation had started and only a cadre of just over 40 officers and men was in the early summer of 1919 going to be officially welcomed back to Reading.

The first months of 1919 were spent for the most part either in battlefield clearance east of Douai or in sporting competitions. The former activity included the removal of debris and discarded equipment; the latter the defeat in the final of the divisional football tournament at the hands of the 9th Essex by 3:1.

On 4 February the battalion, under Lieutenant-Colonel Goodland, was presented with its King's Colour by the Prince of Wales, who in his address recalled the battalion's service:

Men of the 5th Battalion engaged on battlefield clearance. The Battalion Commander, Lieutenant-Colonel H T Goodland, is in the centre of the picture

'You were raised in August 1914, and came out to France in the 12th Division in May 1915. Since that date, in addition to much hard fighting in minor engagements and long periods of strenuous work in the trenches, you have taken a conspicuous part in the following battles:-Loos, Somme 1916, Arras, Cambrai, Somme 1918, Epéhy and the German retreat to the Scheldt, which culminated in the final victory of our arms.'

5th Battalion cinema and recreation room built in the winter of 1918–1919 from materials left behind by the German army

In early June the cadre of four officers and 38 men, led by Lieutenant-Colonel Goodland, went by rail to Dunkirk where they spent a week before sailing for Southampton. They arrived in Reading at 5.00pm on 18 June to be welcomed outside the Great Western Railway station by their first Commanding Officer, Colonel F W Foley, representing the Lord Lieutenant.

Among their number were 16 men of the battalion who had enlisted in 1914. These 'originals' included Private Harry Harding whose memoir of service life has provided authentic glimpses of the men's experiences, including these reflections on the final days:

'On the principle of first in, first out, I could have gone home, but decided as one of the originals to finish my service with the cadre. With the departure of all the troops except the cadre, we settled down to the happiest six months of my life. A few days were spent at Dunkirk, our cadre being a microcosm of the largest British army ever assembled. We had achieved victory in what was understood to be the war to end war.'

After a civic reception at the Town Hall, the battalion's Colours were taken in procession into St Laurence's Church where they were consecrated by the Canon and placed in the Sanctuary, to be hung over the lectern. The ceremony over, the men were taken back to the Town Hall for refreshments and on to Brock Barracks where, as the local press recorded, 'they were royally entertained for the rest of the evening'.

The life of the 5th Battalion thus ended where it had started, four years and ten months earlier.

8th Battalion

Having spent the last few days of the war quietly in their billets at Le Cateau, the 8th Battalion paraded in the town on Armistice Day and were addressed by their Commanding Officer.

Thereafter they moved in stages to Beaurevoir, west of Arras, where they too were engaged in battlefield clearance. This was the period which the historian of the 18th Division described as 'the dull days of gathering up abandoned wire and derelict corrugated iron, and carting away unused shells'.

On 2 December the battalion took part in 18th Division's final review where over 11,000 officers and men were addressed by their Divisional Commander, Major-General R P Lee. He recalled the names of their principal engagements:

> 'The Division has taken part in most of the great battles from the Somme in 1916 down to the Armistice: the Ancre, Arras, Flanders, The Retreat from the Oise, the Defence of Amiens and lastly the 100 Days' Victory.'

For the men of the Royal Berkshires present, the names from 1916 and 1917 would have been a reminder of what their colleagues in the disbanded 6th Battalion had experienced.

On 1 February the battalion was presented with the King's Colour by the General Officer Commanding XIII Corps, Lieutenant-General P O N Morland.

At the end of that month a draft of two officers and 257 men was sent to join the Army of Occupation which under the terms of the armistice was to be stationed in the Rhineland. The battalion diarist noted:

> 'The departure of the draft emphasised very clearly the impending dissolution of the battalion and although many men had already left for demobilisation, the loss of two officers and 257 men was the unkindest cut of all.'

The first draft for demobilisation had in fact left the battalion as early as 24 December 1918. These were 20 men who were going to become miners. By early February a further 250 had returned home. A field return on 28 March recorded that battalion strength was 20 officers and 90 other ranks. On 12 April 1919 the battalion was reduced to cadre and the remaining men were transferred to the 3rd Battalion.

There appears to have been no official homecoming for the battalion or indeed for any other of 18th Division. Perhaps the final words for the men of the 8th – and for those of the 5th and 6th Battalions – might come from the division's historian, Captain G H F Nichols, himself a serving member. He speaks for the 18th Division but his words must have equal force for the 12th:

> 'The 18th was a Division that was born with the war and died with the war. Its truest, most enduring associations were with the torn

soil and the wrecked towns of Northern France. Here was a plain English Division that did its duty, took pride in being competent, groused sometimes at the calls made upon it, but forgot hardships and disappointments in the glowing moments of test.'

The Battalions' Colours

All regular and territorial battalions of the BEF's infantry regiments were presented with two sets of Colours, one a King's Colour and the other a Regimental Colour. When the Kitchener battalions were formed they became part of the regimental 'family' but because of wartime restrictions they did not initially receive Colours. Towards the end of the war however it was considered just and right that the Kitchener battalions should be able to display their battle honours on a King's Colour and these were duly presented: to the 5th and 8th Battalions early in 1919 and to representatives of the disbanded 6th Battalion in August 1920.

The 5th Battalion's Colour was laid up on 18 June 1919 in St Laurence's Church, Reading and it can still be seen there today, flanked by the Colours of the 49th Regiment of Foot which were carried from 1860 to 1889.

The Colours of both the 6th and the 8th Battalions were deposited in St Giles Church, Reading but are not there today. Attempts made to locate them have failed and any news of their present whereabouts would be most gratefully received by the authors and by the regiment.

Appendix I

Local men who served with the battalions in 1918

5th Battalion

**Private
John Bates Bushell** MM

Private Bushell was one of five sons of Mr & Mrs A Bushell of Church Street, Theale. He lived with his wife Edith at 1 Jubilee Cottages, Holyport, Maidenhead. On 12 May 1918 he and Sergeant Frank Varney of Faringdon followed a German raiding party back into No Man's Land and brought in a wounded German officer whose capture was useful for identification of the unit. Pte Bushell was awarded the Military Medal for this action whilst Sgt Varney received the Distinguished Conduct Medal.

Pte Bushell died, aged 33, of influenza on 3 November 1918 and is buried in St Sever Cemetery Extension Rouen, Plot VIII Row L Grave 18.

**Sergeant
Thomas Henry Davies** DCM

Sergeant Davies was the son of Mrs Emma Eden of 94 Grove Road, Windsor. He was awarded the Distinguished Conduct Medal for gallantry during a night raid when he took over command after his officer had been wounded, reached the enemy line and brought back several prisoners. He then went out again three times through a heavy barrage and brought in wounded men from No Man's Land.

He was killed, aged 24, on 22 August 1918 during the attack on the village of Méaulte and is buried in Méaulte Military Cemetery, Grave E17.

**Private
Wilfred John Gosling**

Private Gosling was the son of Mr & Mrs J Gosling, his father being the Keeper of Reading Town Hall. Before joining the 5th Battalion he served with the Berkshire Yeomanry. He died of wounds, aged 19, on 7 April 1918 and is buried in Étaples Military Cemetery, Plot XXXIII Row E Grave 19.

**Private
Albert Hathaway**

Private Hathaway was the son of Mr & Mrs E Hathaway of Burghfield Common and the husband of Rose Clara Hathaway of 158 Way Street, Basingstoke. He joined the Royal Berkshire Regiment three weeks after the outbreak of war and went with the 7th Battalion to Salonika where he served for almost two years. After a spell in England on sick leave, during which he married, he was posted to the 5th Battalion in France on 21 December 1917.

He was killed in action, aged 29, on 5 April 1918 and is commemorated on the Pozières Memorial to the Missing.

**Corporal
Francis William Hermon MM**

Corporal Hermon lived at 18 Bosier Square, Coley Street, Reading. He went to France with the 5th Battalion in May 1915 and served with them throughout the war, being demobilised on 8 April 1919. He was awarded the Military Medal and received the decoration at a ceremony held in Reading Market Place in July 1918.

**Sergeant
Frederick Holmes MM**

Sergeant Holmes was the eldest son of Mr & Mrs Holmes of Redfield Cottages, Newbury, who had seven sons and one son-in-law serving in the forces. He went to France with the 5th Battalion in May 1915 and was wounded three times and gassed twice. He was awarded the Military Medal for gallantry during the operations from 8-12 August 1918. He was discharged on 26 June 1919.

**Captain
Clifford Angus Mallam MC & Bar**

Captain Mallam was the youngest son of Dr G B & Mrs Mallam of Hall Place, Sparsholt, Berkshire. He was educated at Epsom College and Keble College Oxford. He was commissioned into the Royal Berkshire Regiment in 1915 and went to France on 17 March 1916. He served for three years as adjutant of the 5th Battalion, was mentioned in dispatches and was awarded the Military Cross for gallantry at the Battle of Cambrai in November 1917. The Bar to his Military Cross was awarded, in the words of the official citation dated 11 January 1919:

> 'For conspicuous gallantry and devotion to duty during an advance. When the situation was obscure and a gap was reported to exist in our lines, he went out under heavy shell fire to reconnoitre and brought back most valuable information which enabled the battalion to move forward and fill the gap.'

On 28 October 1918 the battalion was heavily shelled and Capt Mallam was wounded. On the following day it was reported that he had died of his wounds. He is buried in Douai British Cemetery, Cuincy.

**Corporal
Joseph J Sargeant DCM MM**

Corporal Sargeant of 15 Easthampstead Road, Wokingham served in the 6th Battalion until it was disbanded in February 1918 when he was transferred to the 5th Battalion. Whilst serving with the 6th Battalion he was awarded the Military Medal. With the 5th Battalion he was awarded the Distinguished Conduct Medal, the official citation dated 23 October 1918 reading:

> 'For conspicuous gallantry and devotion to duty during a night raid. Being left with only two men in his section he led them to the entrance of a dug-out where he was met by a volley from the enemy crouched in the entrance. He sent one man round each flank and attacked the dug-out with bombs, driving the enemy to the bottom. He then went down and brought up two prisoners, the remainder of the garrison having been killed. After the withdrawal signal had been given he returned through the barrage and brought in three wounded men.'

**Private
Henry J Tanner MM**

Private Tanner of 52 Granby Gardens, Reading served in the 5th and the 8th Battalions of the Royal Berkshire Regiment. He was wounded three times and was awarded the Military Medal.

Appendix I

Warrant Officer
William Tilbury MC COL

Warrant Officer Tilbury was the eldest son of Mr & Mrs W Tilbury of Clematis House, Hurley. At the age of 15 he became a recruit in the 1st Battalion of the Royal Berkshire Regiment and five years later he was on active service in the South African War. He was then sent to India. During his service with the 5th Battalion in the First World War he was mentioned in dispatches and awarded the Military Cross and the Belgian Chevalier de L'Ordre Leopold.

At the end of the war he returned as Regimental Sergeant-Major with the cadre of 5th Battalion. He was later commissioned with the rank of captain and served in the Assam Civil Service as Assistant Commissioner of Police. He died of malaria at the age of 54.

Sergeant
Frank Varney DCM MM & Bar

Sergeant Varney of Stanford in the Dale, Faringdon, served throughout the war with the 5th Battalion and was awarded his Military Medal for gallantry during operations at Monchy le Preux in July 1917. He won the Bar to this medal for his conduct during the German attack on the battalion's positions near Albert on 5 April 1918. A month later an enemy patrol entered the battalion's trenches. They were repulsed and Sergeant Varney pursued them into No Man's Land, bringing back with him a German officer. For this he was awarded the Distinguished Conduct Medal, the official citation reading:

> 'For conspicuous gallantry and devotion to duty. When three of the enemy tried to drag one of his men over the parapet, he bombed and scattered them. He then went out into No Man's Land under heavy fire and brought in a German officer, thus securing a very valuable identification.'

8th Battalion

**Private
Alfred Gilbert Allen**

Private Allen of 56 Filey Road, Reading was the youngest of seven brothers who served in the forces during the war. He was killed in action, aged 18, on 23 October 1918 during an attack near Le Cateau. He is commemorated on the Vis-en-Artois Memorial to the Missing.

**Private
Frederick Bailey MM & Bar**

Private Bailey of 14 Fairfield Cottages, Burnham was a professional at Datchet Golf Club before enlisting in August 1915. He went to France on 1 January 1916 and in August of that year was awarded the Military Medal for carrying despatches through heavy enemy shell fire during an attack north of Bazentin le Petit. The Bar to his Military Medal was awarded for the assistance he gave to his Battalion Commander, Lieutenant-Colonel Dewing, during the German attack on the battalion's positions at Hangard Wood on 4 April 1918. Col Dewey was wounded and had to leave his headquarters. Whilst doing so, helped by Pte Bailey, he was shot through the head and killed instantly.

**Private
George Peter Baldwin**

Private Baldwin was born in Windsor and lived at 6 Clifton Cottages, Eton Wick with his wife and two children. He was 32 at the outbreak of war but enlisted as a volunteer in the 6th Battalion and went to France in August 1915. On the disbandment of the 6th Battalion in February 1918 he was transferred initially to the 18th Entrenching Battalion but by April he was serving with the 8th Battalion. He is reported to have been killed in action on 24 April 1918, although the Battalion War Diary makes no mention of casualties on that date. His place of burial suggests that he was perhaps killed on 4 April during the battalion's counter attack at Hangard Wood.

He is buried in Hangard Wood British Cemetery, Plot I Row D Grave 6.

**Private
Edwin George Farr**

Private Farr of The Limes, Western Avenue, Woodley was educated at Reading Blue Coat School. He served with the 8th Battalion throughout the war, going to France with them in August 1915 and being demobilised on 7 June 1919.

**Sergeant
Stanley Nelson Gordon Giddings**

Sergeant Giddings, of 4 Wichcombe Terrace, Kings Road, Newbury was the son of Mr & Mrs L Giddings also of Newbury. Before joining the army he worked at the Newbury GWR station. He enlisted on 7 September 1914 and went as corporal to France in August 1915. He died, aged 23, at a Casualty Clearing Station on 7 April 1918 of wounds received in action during the opening days of the German offensive. He left a widow who at the time was living at Penshurst, West Street, Newbury.

He is buried in Picquigny British Cemetery, Row G Grave 9.

**Corporal
Percy George Holloway MM**

Corporal Holloway was the second son of Mr & Mrs G Holloway of 102 Beecham Road, Reading and was a postman before enlisting. He died of wounds, aged 24, and is buried in Daours Communal Cemetery Extension, Plot IV Row E Grave 5.

**Private
Frederick Ernest Lewendon**

Private Lewendon was the son of Mrs Davis of Fairhaven, Spencers Wood, Reading. He lived with his wife and son at 25 Howard Street, Reading. He was killed on Easter Sunday, 31 March 1918, near the village of Gentelles, south-east of Amiens. The battalion was not in action on that day, but according to the regimental historian four men were killed and 25 wounded, presumably by shell fire. Pte Lewendon is commemorated on the Pozières Memorial to the Missing.

Their Duty Done

Sergeant
Herbert Frederick George Lunnon MM

Sergeant Lunnon was the son of Mr & Mrs GH Lunnon of 35 Chapel Street, Marlow and was educated at the Marlow Church of England School. Before the war he was an apprentice at the Marlow Branch of International Stores and he initially enlisted in the Oxford & Buckinghamshire Light Infantry. He was wounded at the Battle of Loos in September 1915, thereafter working at a camp in England as a gas instructor. Having risen to the rank of sergeant he was passed fit for active service again and joined the 8th Battalion in France on 5 August 1918.

He was killed in action, aged 22, on 28 August 1918 during the attack on Bernafay and Trônes Woods and is buried in Longueval Road Cemetery, Row J Grave 3.

Second Lieutenant
Charles William Moss

Second Lieutenant Moss was the only son of Mr & Mrs C Moss of Hesketh Lodge, 304 Kings Road, Reading and before the war was on the London staff of Messrs Huntley & Palmer, living with his wife at 144 Beech Hill Road, Highams Park, Chingford. He enlisted as a private in the London Regiment in June 1916 and went with them to France. He was subsequently transferred to the Royal Dublin Fusiliers, being recommended by his Commanding Officer for a commission which he received after a period of home service in January 1918. He then joined the 8th Battalion in France on 17 April 1918.

He was killed in action, aged 30, on 8 August 1918 and is buried in Beacon Cemetery, Plot IV Row C Grave 4.

Corporal
Charles Henry Ostridge

Corporal Ostridge, of 45 Orts Road, Reading, was employed before the war at Huntley & Palmers factory. He was initially reported as missing after the attack on 8 August 1918 but it was later confirmed that he had been killed in action. He is buried in Beacon Cemetery, Plot III Row G Grave 20.

Appendix I

**Private
EJ Pocock** MM

Private Pocock, of 55 Sherman Place, Reading, was awarded the Military Medal for bravery and devotion to duty whilst serving as a stretcher bearer. He survived the war and lived in Reading until his death in January 1975.

**Lieutenant
Charles Edward Boulderson Rogers** MC

Lieutenant Rogers was the elder son of Mr & Mrs G E B Rogers of Kendrick Rise, Reading and was educated at Wellington College. He was commissioned into the Royal Berkshire Regiment in October 1914. On 6 March 1915 he married Miss Jane Walker Pike, daughter of Mr & Mrs S Pike of St Clair, Tilehurst Road, Reading. He was awarded the Military Cross in 1918, the official citation dated 23 April reading:

'For conspicuous gallantry and devotion to duty. He led a party of thirty men to attack an enemy post which he had previously located. The enemy, in considerable strength, unexpectedly opened a heavy fire with rifle grenades and trench mortars from an advanced position. Having silenced the trench mortars and broken up an enveloping movement by rapid fire he resolutely led his party forward and forced the enemy to retire. He showed great dash and presence of mind under heavy fire and exercised fine control over his men.'

**Lance-Corporal
George Sparrow** MM

Lance-Corporal Sparrow of 158 Ock Street, Abingdon was one of two battalion runners on the first day of the German offensive who tried to get in touch with the front line units. They went though the enemy barrage and made towards 'D' Company in Magpie Wood. Before reaching the wood they met German troops and had to turn back. L/Cpl Sparrow was awarded the Military Medal for bravery on 24 August 1918 in the action at La Boisselle. He was demobilised on 6 February 1919.

Company Sergeant-Major William John Spokes DCM

Company Sergeant-Major Spokes of Twyford went to France with the 5th Battalion in May 1915 and was subsequently transferred to the 8th Battalion. He had served in the Royal Navy before the war. On 21 March 1918 he led an attack down Seine Alley, a communication trench, after two officers, Major D Tosetti and Lieutenant S A G Harvey, had been killed. This attack successfully cleared the way for the withdrawal of the battalion, and for the gallantry and determination he displayed on this occasion, C S M Spokes was awarded the Distinguished Conduct Medal. He survived the war and died in 1973.

Lance-Corporal John Holder Weait

Lance-Corporal Weait was the son of Mr & Mrs A Weait of 20 Watlington Street, Reading. He was killed in action, aged 22, on 8 August 1918 and he is commemorated on the Vis-en-Artois Memorial to the Missing.

Appendix I

Appendix II

The Hudson Family

A TRIBUTE FROM WING COMMANDER
T F H HUDSON (RTD)

The service careers of three members of the Hudson family, Thomas, Arthur and Noel, have featured prominently in our series of booklets. We are very pleased to be able to include here in the last volume a short tribute from Thomas's son, Wing Commander T F H Hudson (rtd), who has from the outset been most generous in his support of our project.

Four of the sons of the Reverend Thomas Hudson, Rector of Great Shefford, served in the Great War. They were all educated at St Edward's School, Oxford, of which their father had previously been headmaster.

The eldest son, Eric, born in 1886, was a regular officer in the Worcestershire Regiment. As a captain he took part in their famous action in October 1914 when they recaptured the vital position of Gheluvelt from the Prussian Guard and thus saved the whole British line. As a result of wounds received later he spent the latter part of the war in West Africa and he eventually retired with the rank of major.

The other three sons all served with the Kitchener battalions of the Royal Berkshire Regiment. Thomas, the second son, born in 1888, went up to Selwyn College, Cambridge, where he was good enough to be in the running for a Blue at both rugby and rowing. He played rugby for the Harlequins alongside Ronnie Poulton-Palmer, the England star of his day who was killed in May 1915 as a captain in the 1/4th Battalion of the Royal Berkshire Regiment.

Originally a schoolmaster, Thomas decided to go into the Church and therefore proceeded to Westcott House, the Cambridge theological college. He was there in 1914 but immediately joined the Royal Berkshires, later becoming captain and adjutant of the 5th Battalion. He was due to go on leave as his wife was expecting a child, but he chose to stay with his battalion for the impending attack at Loos. He was killed there on 13 October 1915. His widow died in 1987 at the age of 101.

The third son, Arthur, born in 1891, was at Keble College, Oxford, in 1914. He had played for the Harlequins at the same time as Thomas and also immediately joined the Royal Berkshire Regiment. He was killed as a captain with the 6th Battalion on 31 July 1917, during the opening stage of the Third Battle of Ypres. He was posthumously mentioned in dispatches for his conduct on that day.

The fourth son, Noel, born in 1894, was a Scholar of Christ's College, Cambridge, and he likewise joined the Royal Berkshires on the outbreak of war. He first served with the 6th Battalion alongside his brother Arthur and went on to have an outstanding war record. He rose to temporary command of a brigade at the age of 24, having commanded the 8th Battalion and been awarded the DSO & Bar and the MC & Bar within a period of 18 months.

During his time as Battalion Commander Noel enjoyed the distinction of having Colonel Kermit Roosevelt, son of President Theodor Roosevelt, attached to him for combat experience. The friendship formed between the two men was to bear fruit later. After the war Noel too went to Westcott House and whilst there kept up the family tradition of playing for the Harlequins, despite having been wounded in action several times.

Noel went on to have an equally outstanding career in the Church. Originally a curate in a very poor parish in Leeds (where he played rugby for Yorkshire), he became vicar of a similar parish in Newcastle in 1926. From there he was appointed Bishop of Labuan and Sarawak in 1931, being recalled seven years later to become Secretary of the Society for the Propagation of the Gospel.

In 1940 he was sent by the Archbishop of Canterbury to the United States to ask the American Episcopal Church if they could help fund Anglican overseas missions during the war. Knowing of the high regard in which Noel was held by the Roosevelt family, the Americans insisted on giving far more than the Archbishop had asked for.

A year later Noel was appointed Bishop of Newcastle and in 1957 he was translated to the Bishopric of Ely, which was particularly gratifying for a Cambridge man. He retired in 1963 and died in 1970.

The commemorative plaque to Noel Hudson in Ely Cathedral

Appendix II

Appendix III

Prisoners of War

One of the striking features of the 1918 campaigns was the large number of prisoners of war who were taken as a result of swift penetration made on the opening days of an offensive. This was particularly true of the German March Offensive when, according to Martin Middlebrook, some 21,000 British soldiers went into captivity on the first day.

In what follows we attempt to reflect this aspect of the war through the experiences of men who served with the two Royal Berkshire battalions, predominantly those of the 8th Battalion who took the first impact of the German attack on 21 March.

We begin with a personal account and then move into short biographies of some of the local men who became prisoners of war. For two of these, Lieutenant John Edward Mecey and Sergeant Stanley William Tarrant, we have been able to bring together rather more material than for the others and they are given greater prominence.

Sergeant Tarrant's story is of particular interest, partly because he was taken prisoner as early as 1916, but more significantly because we have had the good fortune to meet his daughter, Mrs Mary Gyngell, who very kindly gave us access to family papers and to family memories.

IN A GERMAN PRISONER OF WAR CAMP

The *Reading Mercury* of 7 December 1918 carried an article entitled 'Home from Germany' which contains one of the very few accounts from local men about their experience as prisoners of war and which is of particular value for the glimpse it affords of the situation in Germany at the end of the war.

The main correspondent was Lieutenant Norman Langston, youngest son of Mrs E Langston of Cork Street, Reading. The article explains how Lt Langston, along with fellow officers of the 8th Battalion and a large number of men, was taken prisoner on 21 March 1918. They were, according to the report, taken first to a position just behind the German lines at St Quentin where they were held for 36 hours without food. Their eventual destination was a camp near the town of Rastatt in southern Germany. Lt Langston described the conditions:

> 'Here we had three months' starvation. Our daily fare was two plates of thin soup and one fifth of a loaf of bread a day. It was rather a pathetic sight to see your brother officers getting so appreciably thinner. At Rastatt they treated us like dogs.'

From Rastatt the majority of the officers were sent to a camp at Hesepe in northern Germany. Here they began to receive parcels from home, most of which at first arrived intact. Later many of them were apparently rifled, but so cleverly that it was difficult to see where they had been opened. Lt Langston's impression was that the German guards received no better rations than the prisoners did. He sketched in other aspects of daily life:

> 'At first we tried to study, but it was difficult to keep it up. We played hockey with walking sticks, but eventually obtained some English hockey sticks for which we paid 20 Marks which would be equal to about 20 shillings in peacetime. A small basket cost us £2-5 shillings and I paid 27 Marks for a suitcase made of cardboard and thin material outside. We had a camp committee headed by Major Leslie Faber and they saw that grievances were remedied. A great deal depends upon the commandant of the camp, and the camp at Hesepe was not so bad.'

The last two months of captivity were spent in Cologne where the treatment was better, the reason being according to Lt Langston that the Germans became nicer as the tide of war turned against them. The end of the war in fact brought with it revolutionary activity in many parts of Germany, leading to the formation of local Soldiers' and Workers' Councils as the established order collapsed. The consequences were noted by Lt Langston:

> 'When the Soldiers' Councils took over control we used to be allowed into the town and to visit the cafés. We had a good time and people invited us to their homes. On being released we left Cologne which was beflagged for the returning German soldiers whom the people seemed to look on as unbeaten. We came down the Rhine on a 9,000-ton vessel which carried 160 officers and 1,300 men. They did us very well on the boat, and at Rotterdam everything that a man could want – a change of uniform, razors, parcels etc – was provided by the British government. We could not have been treated better. As we sailed up the Humber to Hull the sirens were sounded and a very cordial welcome was accorded us.'

Lt Langston arrived in England on 28 November 1918 and was demobilised on 5 June 1919.

OTHER LOCAL MEN WHO BECAME
PRISONERS OF WAR

**Private
William Eustace**
Private Eustace, the son of Mr and Mrs Tom Eustace of Spencers Farm Cottages, Maidenhead, was taken prisoner on 21 March 1918 when serving with the 8th Battalion. He died on 26 August 1918, aged 20, of dysentry and heart failure at Hautmont, near Maubeuge. He is buried in Hautmont Communal Cemetery, Plot V Row D Grave 4.

**Captain
David John Footman**
Captain Footman was born at Watchfield, Berkshire on 17 September 1895, the son of the Reverend John & Mrs Footman. He joined the 8th Battalion on 22 October 1915 and was awarded the Military Cross for gallantry when he led a successful raid on the German trenches on 3 May 1916. In July of that year he was wounded by shrapnel and after treatment in England he rejoined the battalion in April 1917. For gallantry shown during the Third Battle of Ypres he was awarded the Belgian Croix de Guerre.

He was reported missing after the German attack on 21 March 1918 and was initially thought to have died of wounds. On 18 May 1918 the local press confirmed that he was a prisoner of war in Germany. He returned to England in December with the group of fellow officers from his battalion.

Educated at Marlborough College, he went to Oxford University in March 1919 but left without taking a degree. After ten years in the Consular Service he worked in the Balkans for HMV and then joined the Foreign Office. He was a member of MI6 for 20 years until his retirement in 1953. Thereafter he was responsible for establishing a Russian Centre at St Antony's College Oxford before he retired for a second time in 1962 at the age of 67.

Captain Footman died on 12 October 1983.

**Private
Joseph Sidney Freeman**
Private Freeman was the son of George Freeman of 4 Beansheaf Terrace, Wallingford and husband of Mrs L M Freeman of 3 Goldsmiths Lane, Wallingford. He served with the 8th Battalion and died of pneumonia, aged 25, on 29 June 1918 whilst a prisoner of war in Germany. He is buried in Berlin South-Western Cemetery, Plot 1 Row A Grave 3.

**Captain
Cyril Gentry-Birch MC**
Captain Gentry-Birch was born in September 1892, the only child of Mr & Mrs J Gentry-Birch of Caversham, Reading, and was educated at York House School and University College Reading. In June 1915 he married Elsie Jeanette Girdler.

He distinguished himself with the 8th Battalion at the Battle of Loos on 25 September and 13th October 1915, being awarded the Military Cross for his gallantry. As Commanding Officer of 'A' Company he was initially reported as killed in action on 21 March 1918, but a later communication from the War Office stated that he was a slightly wounded prisoner of war in German hands. He was with Lt Langston and fellow officers in the camps at Rastatt, Hesepe and Cologne and was repatriated with them.

Captain Gentry-Birch died at Finchampstead on 31 July 1985.

Lance-Corporal
Ernest Clargo Grant

Lance-Corporal Grant was the son of Mr & Mrs C Grant of The Mount, Hurst, Twyford. He served with the Devonshire and London Regiments before joining the 8th Battalion of the Royal Berkshire Regiment. He was taken prisoner in August 1918 and died on 29 September of inflammation of the lung whilst in the War Hospital at Le Cateau. He is buried in Le Cateau Military Cemetery, Plot 1 Row B Grave 43.

Second Lieutenant
WCA Hanney

Second Lieutenant Hanney came from a Reading family which had a number of connections with the Royal Berkshire Regiment. On 21 March 1918 whilst in charge of the right of 'D' Company's line he reported that the Germans had entered the front line trenches but that he was holding out. Later that day he was taken prisoner having been wounded in the face by shrapnel. He was taken to the internment camp at Rastatt where the wound was treated. He returned from captivity on 7 December 1918.

Lieutenant
Edward John Mecey

Lieutenant Mecey was the eldest son of Mr & Mrs E Mecey of High St Thatcham. Educated at Reading School, he was a law student when war broke out. He enlisted in the Royal Fusiliers and was commissioned into the Royal Berkshire Regiment in August 1916. Whilst commanding 'D' Company of the 8th Battalion on 21 March 1918 he was taken prisoner and was transported with fellow officers to Rastatt where he remained until his repatriation in December 1918.

Lt Mecey's formal statement of the circumstances which led to his capture is lodged with his personal papers in the Public Record Office. Dated 15 January 1919, the statement conveys much of the confusion which reigned on the battlefield during the first hours of the German attack on 21 March 1918:

'I was in command of 'D' Company in the front line and on the evening of 20 March 1918 was obliged to leave Battle Company HQ to have my head dressed owing to an injury caused by a beam falling on me from a dug-out entrance. A platoon officer was personally sent by the adjutant to take my place temporarily. At about 4.30 – 5.00am on 21 March the enemy barrage commenced and with it a large quantity of gas. I immediately tried to make my way back to Battle HQ but was lost in the fog. Later I made a second unsuccessful attempt, being out with an orderly for more than an hour, and was obliged to get into a trench on account of the barrage. Shortly after this, the officer who had taken my place came in wounded and reported the position blown in by shell fire and nearly all the men casualties. Consequently I decided to remain at Company HQ as all communication was now cut. Here we were able to make a stand for some time but finally, having no more bombs and ammunition running out, I decided to make my way to posts manned by the support company in advance of Battalion HQ. We had been surrounded but most of us were able to get out owing to the fog. On my way to this position I and a few men with me were surrounded by a large number of the enemy, who appeared suddenly out of the fog before we had an opportunity of making any resistance. I consider our capture was solely due to the denseness of the fog. We were unable to see our own trench-mortar SOS and totally unable to distinguish any object until almost upon it, while the fog seemed to deaden all minor sounds.'

Lt Mecey was also involved in a mystery surrounding the fate of a fellow officer, Lieutenant Frank Mariner Sumpster of 253 Oxford Road, Reading. On 21 March 1918 Lt Sumpster was attached to the 53rd Trench Mortar Battery which was in action with the 8th Royal Berkshires near their front line position at Magpie Wood. In a letter which Lt Mecey sent to a member of his family whilst in captivity he was reported to have written: 'Sumpster is here with us, wounded rather severely but otherwise cheerful.'

However no official confirmation of Lt Sumpster's status as a prisoner of war followed and early in 1919 the Army Council sought evidence from members of the battalion who had been with him on the morning of 21 March 1918. Depositions in Lt Sumpster's personal file held in the Public Record Office include a statement from a stretcher bearer, Private T Vanderplank, who had found Lt Sumpster badly wounded and tried to bandage him. Pte Vanderplank was himself then taken prisoner, convinced that Lt Sumpster had only a very short time to live. This account was considered by the Army Council to be insufficient evidence of death, although it corroborated a statement made by Second Lieutenant W V Heale of 'D' Company on 29 July 1918:

'Lt Sumpster was badly wounded by a bomb in leg and hand. We were in a quarry in Magpie Wood and after telling a stretcher bearer to attend to him, I saw him drag himself into a shelter which was his own Trench Mortar Battery HQ. This was the last I saw of him'.

Evidence which convinced the Army Council that Lt Sumpster had been killed on 21 March 1918 was given by Private G Walters in a statement dated 1 March 1919:

'Lt Sumpster was hit in the middle of the back by a bomb and killed instantly. The body was left in enemy hands.'

A letter from the Army Council to Mrs Sumpster on 18 March 1919 referred to Pte Walters' statement which confirmed its conclusion that her husband had indeed been killed in action.

Lieutenant Sumpster is commemorated on the Pozières Memorial to the Missing.

Private
William E Millson
Private Millson was the son of Mr & Mrs E Millson of Slade Gate, Pangbourne and served in 'B' Company of the 8th Battalion. He died, aged 27, of dysentry on 29 May 1918 whilst in captivity. He is buried in Annois Communal Cemetery, Plot 1 Row B Grave 18.

Private
Henry John Radbourne
Private Radbourne was the son of Mr and Mrs J Radbourne of Stockcross, Newbury. He went to France with the 8th Battalion in August 1915 and was wounded and taken prisoner at the Battle of Loos. He was a prisoner of war for over three years and died, aged 26, on 24 December 1918 whilst being repatriated. He is buried in Riseberga churchyard, Sweden.

Sergeant
Stanley William Tarrant

Sergeant Tarrant was born on 3 September 1893, one of seven children of Mr & Mrs G Tarrant of 17 Tangier Lane, Eton. Before the war he was employed as a boatman at Eton College. One of his elder brothers was wounded during the Gallipoli campaign whilst serving with the navy, another was gassed with the 1st Battalion of the Royal Berkshire Regiment.

Sgt Tarrant enlisted on 25 August 1914 and went to France with the 5th Battalion in May 1915. He was taken prisoner on 3 July 1916 during the attack on Ovillers. This was the action in which the battalion adjutant, Lieutenant Cecil Gold, was killed and Sgt Tarrant often recalled later, according to his family, how he went up to the front line with Lt Gold the day before the attack sharing the knowledge that they both had connections with Eton College, the one as former pupil, the other as employee. After the war Sgt Tarrant frequently took his daughter to see Lt Gold's commemorative plaque in the College cloisters, invariably telling her how lucky he himself had been on 3 July 1916.

After he was captured at Ovillers, Sgt Tarrant was taken first to St Quentin and then to a succession of camps in Germany: at Giessen, Meschede, Soltau and Bohmte. He kept a record in his notebook of the lectures arranged for the men, subjects ranging from 'The Pedigree of the Kaiser' to 'Weather forecasting'. In May 1918 he was moved to The Hague, Holland and was repatriated from there. After the war he resumed his employment at Eton College.

Stanley Tarrant died in 1976. His family dedicated a riverside seat near the Eton College boathouse to his memory.

No. _____
(If replying, please quote above No.)

Army Form B. 104—83A.

Record Office,
_____ Station.
_____ 191 .

[Stamp: INFANTRY RECORD OFFICE 23 SEP. 1916 WARWICK]

SIR OR ~~MADAM~~,

I have to inform you that a report has been received from the War Office to the effect that (No.) *10493* (Rank) *Sgt* (Name) *Tarrant. F.W.* (Regiment) ROYAL BERKSHIRE REGT. is a Prisoner of War *at Giessen 9.8.16*

Should any other information be received concerning him, such information will be at once communicated to you.

Instructions as to the method of communicating with Prisoners of War can be obtained at any Post Office.

I am,
SIR OR ~~MADAM~~,
Your obedient Servant,

[signature]
2nd Lieut. for Br. General
Officer in charge of Records.
i/c Infantry Records.

IMPORTANT.—Any change of your address should be immediately notified to this Office. It should also be notified, if you receive information from the soldier above, that his address has been changed.

(9 38 5) W 13495—5013 80,000 12/15 H W V(P 1361) Forms/B. 104—83A/1

Official confirmation that Sgt Tarrant had been taken prisoner

THE ROYAL BERKSHIRE REGIMENT
PRISONERS OF WAR FUND

The Fund was established to offer practical support to prisoners of war. A Royal Berkshire Regiment Prisoners of War Care Committee, founded in May 1915, took part in its administration. The committee was chaired by Mr William Mount MP. His wife, the signatory of the letter reproduced below to Mrs Tarrant, was the honorary secretary. It is worth recalling that Mr and Mrs Mount's son, Captain Frank Mount, was killed in action at Loos on 13 October 1915 whilst serving with the 5th Battalion of the Royal Berkshire Regiment. He is commemorated on the Loos Memorial to the Missing.

According to a report of the War Care Committee published in *Berkshire and the War* in 1919, 1400 prisoners from the 1st, 2nd, 5th and 8th Battalions of the regiment had been supplied with food parcels every month and with bread every week in the last year of the war. Each prisoner had been sent a complete issue of clothing as soon as he was reported to be in German hands and this was renewed every six months. The total of 1400 prisoners of war in 1918 compares with 260 at the end of 1917 and reflects the impact of the German Spring Offensives.

After 1 November 1918 no more individual bread or food parcels were sent, bulk consignments being despatched by the Central Prisoners of War Committee to a number of centres on the continent. Repatriation of the 140,000 British prisoners in German hands began soon after the armistice negotiations had been completed.

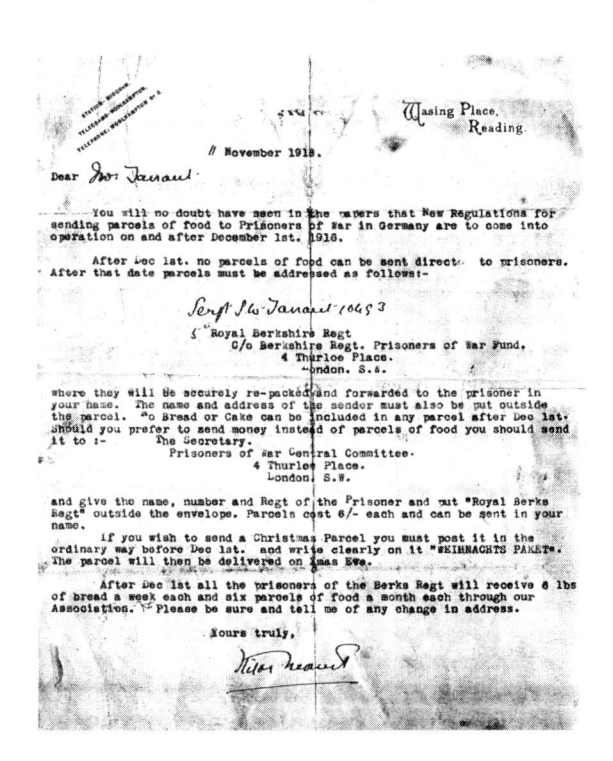

Appendix III

Appendix IV

Visiting the Battlefields today

As in our previous volumes, we have selected two actions for each of the Royal Berkshire battalions to form a short guide to the battlefields today. Criteria for selection have again been accessibility of the terrain and a reasonable certainty that we could identify the locations of the battalions' positions. Very familiar sites have been excluded.

All the sites can easily be approached by car and then explored in more detail on foot. Indispensable maps are the French IGN 1:25000 series.

8th Battalion at Moy 21 March 1918

Map: IGN 2609 ouest St Quentin

Magpie Wood on the sky line as seen fom the D342 La Guingette-Moy road

A direct approach from St Quentin would be via the N44 south to the intersection with the D72 coming from Cerizy and the D342 at La Guingette. From this crossroads a line of four small woods can be seen leading off in a north-easterly direction. The most distant one, on the crest of the slope, is identified on the IGN map as the Bois Frémont. This was Magpie Wood, referred to in Lt Randall's account of the opening hours of the German Spring Offensive. The others were marked on the hand-drawn battalion map as Pinson Copse, Blackbird Copse and Guingette Wood. 'D' Company HQ was in Magpie Wood and Battalion HQ was on the far side of the main road just south of the crossroads.

This piece of countryside seems not to have changed since 1918 and it is well worth exploring on foot for the views it gives of the 21 March battlefield. One footpath leads off to the east some 200 metres north of the crossroads and takes you directly to Magpie Wood. From the high ground to the east of the wood, where the 8th Battalion's front line posts were, you look directly down on to Alaincourt and Moy - exactly as described by Lt Randall. It was here that the battalion's first encounters with the German attacking troops took place.

An alternative walk, giving perhaps better all-round views, leads off from the D342 to Moy. From the La Guingette crossroads the second field track on the left takes you to Pinson Copse. It then joins the footpath coming from the N44 and takes you up to Magpie Wood.

Before leaving the area it is worth calling in at Moy Communal Cemetery on the right of the D342 as it leads down into the town. Here are headstones of British casualties from the cavalry action at Cerizy fought on 28 August 1914 which took place partly on the slopes you have just walked and which is described by Richard Holmes in 'Riding the Retreat'.

**8th Battalion at Gressaire Wood
8 August 1918**

Map: IGN 2408 ouest Albert

The approximate position of the 8th Battalion's action at Gressaire Wood

From Bray-sur-Somme take the D1 west in the direction of Corbie. This is the road which features in the War Diary accounts of actions on 8 August of both the 5th and the 8th Battalions. It is worth stopping at the intersection with the minor road running from Morlancourt down to Chipilly and reached after about five kilometres. From here in clear weather you can look south across the Chipilly Spur and the River Somme over to what was the main battlefield on the opening day of the Final Offensive where the Australian and Canadian Corps launched their attacks. To your left front you have Gressaire Wood, to your right front Malard Wood, both significant features for the 8th Battalion on that day.

Drive down the minor road for 500 metres in the direction of Chipilly and then on to the first track on your left. Almost immediately a footpath appears on your right leading into what on the IGN map is called the Vallée à Carottes. Leave the car here and walk down the path for about 600 metres until you reach a gap in the wood. It was at approximately this point, on the western edge of Gressaire Wood, that the 8th Battalion's advance on 8 August 1918 came to a halt. Lt-Col Hudson was wounded here as he led the attack on German machine gun positions. The battalion's advance had taken them on a line south of the Bray-Corbie road and across the northern tip of Malard Wood.

If, on returning in the car to the D1 you turn towards Corbie, you have immediately on your right the position occupied alongside the road by the 5th Battalion on the afternoon of 8 August 1918 and from which they were relieved in the evening.

5th Battalion at Carnoy 26 August 1918

Map: IGN 2408 est Bray-sur-Somme

View from the D938 over the battlefield east of Carnoy, showing Talus Boisé and Machine Gun Wood

The area we are concerned with lies just to the east of the village of Carnoy and can be approached from Albert on the D938. Take the D254 into the village and then the second exit on the right which ends in a track. Leave the car here and follow the path in the direction of the distinctively long narrow strip of woodland to the north-east. This, named La longue haie on the IGN map, was shown as Talus Boisé on the trench maps and was taken by the 5th Battalion after heavy fighting on 26 August. The battalion's advance on that day had brought

Appendix IV

them on either side of Carnoy.

Just before the southern tip of the wood is reached the track, named on the trench maps as Rail Avenue, branches off to the right. Follow this for 500 metres and across the fields to your left you will see a small copse which the troops knew as Machine Gun Wood (now La Garenne Simon). The 5th Battalion's line on 27 August had its right on this wood and represented the limit of their advance in the actions at Carnoy.

If you drive back up to the D938 and take the left in the direction of Péronne, you could stop after about 1500 metres and look down from the roadside over the ground you have just walked. Talus Boisé and Machine Gun Wood should be clearly visible with Bernafay Wood and Trônes Wood beyond to the north. The village on your right is Maricourt and it was the road from Maricourt to Bernafay Wood which had been the battalion's final objective on 26 August 1918.

5th Battalion at Epéhy 18 September 1918

Map: IGN 2508 est Roisel

The approach road to Epéhy is the D58 and coming from the north-west via Bapaume the village's immediate neighbours are Fins and Heudicourt. The last exit in Epéhy on the left is then the D103 to Honnecourt. Take this and when it crosses the railway line just to the east of the village, stop. There is parking space here on the right. The 5th Battalion line on 18 September was alongside the railway to the left of the road. Ahead and to the right is Tétard Wood, shown but unnamed on the IGN map, and it was the German trenches to the east of the wood which the 5th Battalion captured after hard fighting during the night.

One of the 5th Battalion's objectives on 21 September was Little Priel Farm, still clearly marked on the map today. The easiest

Little Priel Farm today

approach is back through Epéhy on the D103 then left on to the D58 to Ronssoy/Lempire. Take the D28 left through Lempire and just before you go under the A26 motorway call in first at Unicorn Cemetery. Here you will find several headstones of 8th Battalion casualties from their September actions in this area.

The next village ahead is Vendhuile and on the outskirts the first minor road leads off to the left. This takes you directly to Little Priel Farm, which is perhaps best approached on foot to appreciate the terrain. On the bare slopes to the north of the farm were positions familiar to the men after the capture of the farm including the Dados Loop position, a German strong point attacked by the 5th Battalion without success on 24 and 26 September.

Returning to Lempire on the D28 you might look again at the ground on your right between Unicorn Cemetery and the village itself. It was in these fields here that the men of the 8th Battalion fought so hard to clear Yak and Zebra Posts on 19 September 1918.

Appendix V

Casualties and Commemorations

These tables were compiled from several official publications, together with records from the Commonwealth War Graves Commission and the Public Record Office. In some instances, there are variations between the sources in details such as service numbers, spelling of names and dates. In these cases the most probable version has been used. The lists of men killed in action are set out in date order rather than alphabetically. We have chosen this presentation in order to show the impact on the battalions of the actions the men were engaged in during 1918.

kia = killed in action
dow = died of wounds
died = died of other causes

5th Battalion

Date	Name	Rank	Number	Birthplace	Age	Event	Cemetery name
02/01/18	Barlow, Ernest Headley	Pte	25996	Hampstead Norris	37	dow	St Sever Cem Ext
15/02/18	Loxley, Alfred William	Pte	203430	Broughton Hackett	38	dow	Étaples Mil Cem
04/03/18	Rees, Frederick John	Pte	43565	Bristol		kia	Pozières Memorial
08/03/18	Jones, Arthur Inkerman	Pte	21949	Drayton	29	kia	Rue-Pétillon Mil Cem
21/03/18	Bosley, Frederick	Pte	18239	Thatcham		kia	Ploegsteert Memorial
26/03/18	Tanner, William	Pte	16030	Reading		kia	Martinsart Brit Cem
27/03/18	Bansor, Norman Samuel	Pte	41833	Coventry		kia	No entry in CWGC records
	Buckle, Edward Walter	Pte	41824	Beedon		kia	Pozières Memorial
	Coles, William George	L/Sgt	37707	Oldbury	29	kia	Pozières Memorial
	Cooney, Joseph	Pte	202032	Oswaldtwistle	20	kia	Martinsart Brit Cem
	Godfrey, George Robert	Pte	26563	Kennington Berks	38	kia	Pozières Memorial
	Hoare, Edgar	Pte	41626	Kea Cornwall	20	kia	Pozières Memorial
	Miles, Frederick Edmund	Cpl	39042	St Pancras	24	kia	Pozières Memorial
	Paine, George Gordon	Capt			24	dow	Varennes Mil Cem
	Phillips, Percy Owen	Pte	12808	Reading		kia	Pozières Memorial
	Purton, Charles	Pte	33761	Cadley	33	kia	Pozières Memorial
	Seward, Albert	Pte	41822	Reading		kia	Pozières Memorial
	Stone, Horace Gordon	Pte	38678	Ruanminor	19	kia	Pozières Memorial
	Taylor, Frederick	Pte	202999	Birmingham		kia	Martinsart Brit Cem
	Woollatt, Samuel	Pte	203511	Sandwich		kia	Pozières Memorial
28/03/18	Bridges, Francis John	Pte	35856	Clifton on Teme	23	dow	Pozières Memorial
	Dodding, William	Pte	38049	Deanscales	25	kia	Pozières Memorial
	Harris, Reginald	Pte	23596	Devonport	24	kia	Martinsart Brit Cem
	Howie, David Charles	Pte	33676	Cupar	37	kia	Pozières Memorial
	Pickett, Henry Alexander	Pte	41446	Stanford		kia	Pozières Memorial
	Spokes, George Edmund	Pte	10462	Bray	32	kia	Pozières Memorial
29/03/18	Mott, Albert	Pte	203260	Shippon	37	dow	Étaples Mil Cem
	Tegg, Arthur	Pte	11008	Waltham	29	dow	Doullens Comm Cem Ext No1
30/03/18	Fenton, Walter	Pte	36560	Caister	23	kia	Doullens Comm Cem Ext No1
	Horler, Albert James	Pte	43535	Radstock	37	dow	Doullens Comm Cem Ext No1
	Noble, John Stanley	Lieut			19	dow	Doullens Comm Cem Ext No1
02/04/18	Godfrey, William	Sgt	24046	East Hannay	27	dow	St Sever Cem Ext

Date	Name	Rank	Number	Birthplace	Age	Event	Cemetery name
02/04/18	Lloyd, Ernest Henry	Capt	12054		40	dow	St Sever Cem Ext
04/04/18	Cox, Ernest John	Pte	37739	Sonning Common		kia	Pozières Memorial
05/04/18	Addis, Frederick	Cpl	43563	Alveston	30	kia	Pozières Memorial
	Allen, Albert	Pte	203297	Birmingham		kia	Pozières Memorial
	Andrews, Albert George	Pte	20098	Reading		kia	Pozières Memorial
	Binder, George Edward	Pte	35902		22	kia	Pozières Memorial
	Bird, Charles James	Sgt	10275	Abingdon		kia	Pozières Memorial
	Brooker, Leonard	Pte	43546	Sevenoaks	19	kia	Pozières Memorial
	Brown, Alfred Edward	Cpl	18686	Plaistow	18	kia	Pozières Memorial
	Brown, William Frederick	Pte	201425	Reading		kia	Pozières Memorial
	Caveney, John	Pte	202584	Halifax		kia	Pozières Memorial
	Clutterbuck, Arthur	Pte	37712	North Newington	23	dow	Varennes Mil Cem
	Corteen, Arthur Lawton	Pte	43549	Battersea	19	kia	Pozières Memorial
	Cotton, Walter	Cpl	26084	Birmingham	31	kia	Pozières Memorial
	Donaldson, David James	Pte	39046	Battersea	29	kia	Bouzincourt Ridge Cem
	Dudley, Albert	L/Cpl	37367	Birmingham	34	kia	Bouzincourt Ridge Cem
	Dugard, Arthur	Pte	12372	Birmingham	19	kia	Pozières Memorial
	Edmans, Joseph	L/Cpl	9779	Hackney	25	dow	Doullens Comm Cem Ext No1
	Edwards, Oliver Cecil	Pte	37086	Mold		kia	Pozières Memorial
	Elkins, Victor	Pte	200547	Windsor	27	kia	Bouzincourt Ridge Cem
	Epsley, Grigg Francis	Sgt	9309	West Ham	22	kia	Pozières Memorial
	Fisk, John Daniel	Pte	13951	St Lukes Middx	32	kia	Pozières Memorial
	France, Harry	Sgt	32153	Smethwick		kia	Pozières Memorial
	Gordon, William George	L/Cpl	201879	Bristol	28	kia	Pozières Memorial
	Harris, Ernest	Pte	12303	Winson Grn		kia	Bouzincourt Ridge Cem
	Hathaway, Albert	Pte	11789	Reading	29	kia	Pozières Memorial
	Heath, Arthur Joseph	Pte	36068	Dibden	23	kia	Pozières Memorial
	Hodges, George Thomas	Pte	31344	Reading		kia	Pozières Memorial
	Howard, James Frederick	Pte	43556	London	19	kia	Bouzincourt Ridge Cem
	Hudson, Bertie Frederick	Pte	43558	Irthlingborough	19	dow	Bouzincourt Ridge Cem
	Hunt, Victor William	Pte	41816	Stokenchurch		kia	Pozières Memorial
	Johnson, Mark Robert	Pte	41817	Bow	20	kia	Pozières Memorial
	Lane, Frederick Charles	Pte	18482	Lynham		kia	Bouzincourt Ridge Cem
	Lees, Frederick Henry	Pte	39050	Godalming		kia	Pozières Memorial
	Loynes, Sidney John	Pte	16092	South Kensington		kia	Pozières Memorial
	Martin, William	Pte	39336	Henley		kia	Bouzincourt Ridge Cem
	Merry, Lewis Ernest	Pte	202698	Eynsham		kia	Pozières Memorial
	Morton, Charles	Pte	39052	Birkenhead		kia	Pozières Memorial
	Murray, Percy Murray	Pte	41225	Sunninghill	28	kia	Bouzincourt Ridge Cem
	Noon, William	Pte	15589	Froxfield	23	kia	Pozières Memorial
	Nunn, Alfred Henry	Pte	202043	Bristol		kia	Pozières Memorial
	Olley, Charles William	Pte	43561	Croydon	17	kia	Pozières Memorial
	Palmer, Henry Edwards	2/Lieut			34	dow	Bouzincourt Ridge Cem
	Parkes, Thomas	Pte	203207	Belbroughton	35	kia	Pozières Memorial
	Peace, Thomas	Pte	27375	Birmingham	18	kia	Pozières Memorial
	Poole, Albert Charles	Cpl	12045	St Pancras		kia	Pozières Memorial
	Sales, Percy Eric Hudson	Cpl	20193	Reading	24	kia	Pozières Memorial
	Shears, Stanley	Pte	200590	Winterslow	29	kia	Bouzincourt Ridge Cem
	Shepherd, Albert George	Pte	22140	Sparkbrook	21	kia	Pozières Memorial
	Smith, Edward	Pte	19596	Beenham		kia	Pozières Memorial
	Tull, William Horace	Pte	34145	Reading		kia	Bouzincourt Ridge Cem
	Walter, Frederick	Pte	20002	Ham		dow	Pozières Memorial
	Warner, Joseph	Pte	9400	Stoke Newington		kia	Pozières Memorial
	Weller, Arthur Edward	L/Cpl	7419	Reigate	31	kia	Bouzincourt Ridge Cem
	Westwood, Walter Edwin	Pte	36500	Hertford	19	kia	Pozières Memorial
	Willmott, William	Pte	29606	Marston	29	kia	Pozières Memorial
	Wood, George Duncan	Pte	35871	Bermondsey		kia	Pozières Memorial

Date	Name	Rank	Number	Birthplace	Age	Event	Cemetery name
06/04/18	Brown, Frederick George	Pte	34733	Stoke Damerill	19	dow	Gezaincourt Comm Cem Ext
	Veale, Percy Harold	Pte	39044	Bristol	19	dow	Serre Road No 1 Cem
07/04/18	Foord, John Ewart	Pte	43553	Bexhill	19	dow	St Hilaire Cem Ext
	Giles, John Ewart	Pte	41486	Willesden	19	dow	Gezaincourt Comm Cem Ext
	Gosling, Wilfred John	Pte	41825	Caversham	19	dow	Étaples Mil Cem
08/04/18	Brindley, Alfred	Pte	41830	Newbury		dow	Étaples Mil Cem
	Shelton, Sidney Charles	Pte	201749	Shaw		dow	Blighty Valley Cem
11/04/18	Dyde, Charles	L/Sgt	15240	Temple Guiling	27	dow	Étaples Mil Cem
14/04/18	Gray, Herbert	Pte	29621	High Wycombe		dow	Étaples Mil Cem
17/04/18	Coombe, Ralph Higman	Pte	41320	Luxluyan		dow	Étaples Mil Cem
	Rowe, Gilbert JB	2/Lieut			19	dow	Les Baraques Mil Cem
26/04/18	Baker, Henry George	Pte	38690	St Pancras		kia	Mailly Wood Cem
28/04/18	Williams, George	Pte	48501	Bristol	18	kia	Mailly Wood Cem
29/04/18	Hinde, Ernest	Pte	48610	Olney		kia	Mailly Wood Cem
03/05/18	Holmes, Gilbert Dalton	Pte	39047	Bodmin	38	dow	Berlin South Western Cem
04/05/18	Boddy, Edward Frederick	Pte	38075	Bristol	19	dow	Doullens Comm Cem Ext No2
07/05/18	Duley, Arthur James	Pte	25796	Birmingham		dow	Hautrage Mil Cem
	Westlake, George	Pte	43915	Plymouth		kia	Mailly Wood Cem
09/05/18	Snooks, William Arthur	Pte	45098	Smethwick		kia	Mailly Wood Cem
10/05/18	Harrison, James	Pte	27018			dow	Étaples Mil Cem
12/05/18	White, Sidney Albert	Pte	41625	Sheffield	18	dow	Bagneux Brit Cem
17/05/18	Lidster, Alfred George	Pte	33358	Dawlish		died	Berlin South Western Cem
	Parvin, Reginald John	Pte	38641	Blagdon	19	kia	Merville Comm Cem Ext
20/05/18	Rowell, Thomas	2/Lieut				died	Northampton Gen Cem
24/05/18	Jephcott, George James	Pte	203285	Birmingham	21	kia	Pozières Memorial
25/05/18	Austin, Archibald Victor	Pte	48632	Birmingham		kia	Mailly Wood Cem
	Chapman, George William	Pte	39021	Bungay	28	dow	Bagneux Brit Cem
	Constable, Frederick Victor	Pte	48637	Birmingham	18	kia	Pozières Memorial
	Cook, John	Pte	39036	Parkham	22	kia	Pozières Memorial
	Cox, Leonard Bernard	Pte	48701	Penryn	19	kia	Ancre British Cem
	Coxhead, Reginald	Pte	48556	Winterbourne		kia	Pozières Memorial
	Davey, Albert Edward	Pte	48543	Kennerley	19	kia	Pozières Memorial
	Evans, Arthur Alfred	Pte	48559	Great Walley	18	kia	Pozières Memorial
	Evans, Harold Donald	Pte	43884	Gloucester		kia	Pozières Memorial
	Forsey, Edwin Charles	Pte	48709	Chetnole	19	dow	Pozières Memorial
	Hillman, Charles Thomas	Pte	220788	Charlwood		kia	Mailly Wood Cem
	Hughes, Alfred Hugh	Pte	45093	Streatham	18	kia	Mailly Wood Cem
	Hughes, Lewis Barnabas	L/Cpl	48566	Bray		kia	Pozières Memorial
	Kemp, Leslie Frank	L/Cpl	45040	Bursley	19	kia	Pozières Memorial
	Masingham, Harry	Pte	203399	Toulsham		kia	Mailly Wood Cem
	Moore, Charles Tom	Pte	48659	Blandford		kia	Mailly Wood Cem
	Muir, John Murray	Pte	39000	Ceres	37	kia	Mailly Wood Cem
	Newman, Sidney	L/Cpl	202677	Birmingham	30	dow	Acheux British Cem
	Perry, Frank	Pte	38974	Fyfield	25	kia	Pozières Memorial
	Stevens, Frederick David	Pte	38950	Wool, Dorset	28	kia	Pozières Memorial
	Stevens, John	Pte	38976	Lewisham	21	dow	Acheux British Cem
	Trillow, Charles Henry	Sgt	23710	Ingatestone		kia	Pozières Memorial
	Ward, Stanley	Pte	45033	Lechlade	21	kia	Ancre British Cem
	Wilcox, Sidney	Pte	38978	Portland		kia	Pozières Memorial
	Wood, Thomas	Pte	220782		37	dow	Pozières Memorial
26/05/18	Hanney, Alexander Desmond	Pte	48647	Frome	18	dow	Bagneux Brit Cem
27/05/18	Coote, George Bernard	Lieut				kia	No entry in CWGC records
	Dawson, Harold	Pte	35549		30	dow	Birmingham (Witton) Cem
	Lewis, Wilfred James	Sgt	20976	Dalston	33	dow	Favreuil Brit Cem
28/05/18	Osborne, Reginald Ralph	Pte	45683	Long Ashton	19	dow	Doingt Comm Cem Ext
31/05/18	Richards, George Howard	Pte	45048	Ilfracombe		dow	Holy Trinity Churchyard
05/06/18	Poolman, Albert	Pte	37734			dow	Niederzwehren Cem

Appendix V

Date	Name	Rank	Number	Birthplace	Age	Event	Cemetery name
18/06/18	Godfrey, Albert	Pte	43567	Branton	35	died	Péronne Comm Cem Ext
19/06/18	Mitchell, Albert Edward	Pte	38572	Hammersmith	19	kia	Bouzincourt Comm Cem Ext
20/06/18	Barnes, Anthony Joseph	Pte	17698	Wolverhampton		kia	Bouzincourt Comm Cem Ext
	Barrett, Harry George	Pte	17302	Hackney	21	kia	Bouzincourt Comm Cem Ext
	Colston, Ernest Henry	Pte	48555	Rugby	19	kia	Bouzincourt Comm Cem Ext
	Green, William	Pte	11166	Camberwell	24	kia	Bouzincourt Comm Cem Ext
	Turton, Edward	Pte	17188	Poplar	21	kia	Bouzincourt Comm Cem Ext
24/06/18	Griffin, Wallace Ethorne	Pte	43883	Thurmeston	19	dow	Varennes Mil Cem
	Mayman, Roland Lister	Pte	220655	Dewsbury	19	dow	Varennes Mil Cem
26/06/18	Cloke, Cyril Richard	Pte	48696	Thornbury	19	kia	Bouzincourt Comm Cem Ext
	Cornick, Bertie Walter	Pte	48699	Poole		kia	Bouzincourt Comm Cem Ext
	Godwin, Charles Edward	Pte	48270	Alveston	19	kia	Bouzincourt Comm Cem Ext
03/07/18	Rogers, Albert John	L/Cpl	8677	Coldmerholm		died	Valenciennes Comm Cem
	Sutton, William Henry	Pte	50677	Birmingham		kia	Bouzincourt Comm Cem Ext
05/07/18	Williams, Alfred Henry	L/Cpl	43879	Jersey CI	19	dow	St Sever Cem Ext
08/07/18	Dell, Frederick Alfred	Pte	42317	Chalfont	19	kia	Harponville Comm Cem Ext
12/07/18	Prince, Albert Edward	Pte	34094	North Heath	20	died	Tincourt New Brit Cem
23/07/18	Boshell, Frederick Stephen	2/Lieut			26	kia	St Amand Brit Cem
27/07/18	Moore, Thomas	Pte	43887	Moretonhamstead	19	dow	Holy Trinity Churchyard
06/08/18	Perris, Albert Charles	Pte	22608	Great Shefford		died	Roye New Brit Cem
08/08/18	Blake, Alfred Thomas	Pte	19686	Hurst	29	kia	Vis-en-Artois Memorial
	Bowdidge, Arthur Charles	Pte	43917	Okehampton	19	kia	Vis-en-Artois Memorial
	Fyfe, Arthur George	Pte	48715	Exbridge	19	kia	Beacon Cem
	Hill, John	Pte	48568	Ludlow		kia	Beacon Cem
	Robinson, Tom	Pte	38940	Ambleside	19	kia	Beacon Cem
09/08/18	Heard, John Hooper	Pte	38469	Delabole		dow	Pernois Brit Cem
10/08/18	Aston, Robert John	Pte	48547	Snowshill	19	dow	Pernois Brit Cem
11/08/18	Bickers, Edward Coulson	Cpl	48546	Southampton	19	kia	Beacon Cem
	Bradbury, Samuel	Pte	50739	Aston		dow	Pernois Brit Cem
	Plant, Harry	Pte	43859	Wearington		kia	Vis-en-Artois Memorial
	Swain, John	Pte	39463			died	Montigny Comm Cem Ext
12/08/18	Miles, Clarence	Pte	38637	Stafford	19	kia	Ville-sur-Ancre Comm Cem Ext
13/08/18	Heawood, William Henry	L/Cpl	12442	Aston	25	kia	Beacon Cemetery
15/08/18	Darling, George Henry	A/Cpl	25526	Abingdon	37	dow	Terlincthun Brit Cem
16/08/18	Ivett, Daniel	Pte	11084	Bromley by Bow	23	died	Brie British Cem
17/08/18	Booth, Harold	Sgt	41384	Bolton	26	dow	Corbie Comm Cem Ext
18/08/18	Hill, William	Pte	39339	Chalfont St Peters	23	dow	Daours Comm Cem Ext
19/08/18	Swan, Jack	Pte	33690	Ramsgate		kia	Serre Road No 1 Cem
20/08/18	Thomas, Harold Edward	L/Cpl	43896	Birmingham	19	kia	Péronne Road Cem
22/08/18	Barrett, Joseph John	Pte	35596		24	kia	Méaulte Mil Cem
	Davis, Thomas Henry	Sgt	10058	Windsor	24	kia	Méaulte Mil Cem
	Hawkins, Frederick George	Pte	43537	Weston Supermare	26	kia	Méaulte Mil Cem
	Osborne, Leslie Leon	Pte	39015	Brighton	21	kia	Méaulte Mil Cem
23/08/18	Bartley-Dennis, Thomas V	Major				died	Hillingdon Cem
24/08/18	Giles, William Reginald	L/Cpl	43893	Brixham	19	kia	Vis-en-Artois Memorial
	Harrison, Frank Ainsworth	L/Cpl	48725	Brockley	19	dow	Daours Comm Cem Ext
	Rose, John	Pte	37354	Reading	22	dow	Daours Comm Cem Ext
25/08/18	Battrick, Dick	Pte	48553	Swanage		kia	Péronne Road Cem
	Boylan, Harold	Pte	39070	Bristol		kia	Péronne Road Cem
	Bragg, John	Pte	43901	St Austell		kia	Péronne Road Cem
	Cox, Walter	Pte	48636	Enford	18	kia	Péronne Road Cem
	George, Ernest	Pte	17706	Reading		kia	Epéhy Wood Farm Cem
	Gerry, Stanley George	Pte	48561	Wadebridge		kia	Péronne Road Cem
	Martyn, William Frederick	Pte	39152	St Austell		kia	Péronne Road Cem
	Richards, Frederick Charles	Pte	43882	Brixham		kia	Péronne Road Cem
	Sillman, Harry	Pte	38951	Tormanton		kia	Péronne Road Cem
26/08/18	Allum, Godfrey Lewis	Pte	203413	Henley		kia	Péronne Road Cem

Date	Name	Rank	Number	Birthplace	Age	Event	Cemetery name
26/08/18	Astell, Frank Reginald	Pte	220766	Kings Heath	19	kia	Péronne Road Cem
	Barnes, Charles William	Pte	41455		23	kia	Péronne Road Cem
	Barr, John Davis	Pte	48551	Leamington	19	kia	Péronne Road Cem
	Barton, Frederick Harold	Pte	38934	Calne	26	kia	Péronne Road Cem
	Bennett, Joseph Victor	Cpl	220386	Hull		kia	Péronne Road Cem
	Bishop, Walter George	Pte	44784	Gloucester	19	kia	Péronne Road Cem
	Clarke, Patrick	Sgt	16881	Oswaldtwistle		kia	Péronne Road Cem
	Collins, Henry James	Pte	43550	Walworth	19	kia	Péronne Road Cem
	Crook, Frederick James	Pte	202772	Bristol		kia	Péronne Road Cem
	Doherty, Ernest Frederick	Pte	48557	Bristol		kia	Péronne Road Cem
	Edwards, Godfrey	Pte	48706	Penzance	18	kia	Péronne Road Cem
	Fathers, John Walters	Pte	48601	Hethe		kia	Péronne Road Cem
	Hine, Servington	Pte	43900	Ugborough		kia	Péronne Road Cem
	Hooker, Leonard	Pte	38967	Wokingham		kia	Péronne Road Cem
	Howson, Frank Wilfred	Pte	48570	Plymouth	19	kia	Péronne Road Cem
	Jackson, Lionel Arthur	Pte	48571	Upton St Leonards		kia	Péronne Road Cem
	Jenkins, William Stanley	Pte	48655	Southall		kia	Péronne Road Cem
	Kingdom, Reginald	Pte	39500	Bideford	20	kia	Péronne Road Cem
	Knight, Romulus Richard	Pte	11233	Caversham	35	kia	Péronne Road Cem
	Lee, Cyril Ewart	Pte	48572	Dudley	19	kia	St Sever Cem Ext
	Lines, George Henry	Pte	48573	Daventry	19	kia	Péronne Road Cem
	Martin, Sidney Albert	L/Cpl	48626	Exmouth		kia	Péronne Road Cem
	Mitchell, Albert Edward	Pte	48542	Fringford		kia	Péronne Road Cem
	Olds, Arthur James	Pte	48577	Bristol		kia	Péronne Road Cem
	Palmer, Clement Foster	L/Cpl	48619	Devonport		kia	Péronne Road Cem
	Parsons, Stanley Maurice	Pte	48616	Glastonbury	19	kia	Péronne Road Cem
	Perry, Ernest George	Pte	48578	Clifton		kia	Péronne Road Cem
	Pettifer, George	Pte	11514	Windsor		kia	Péronne Road Cem
	Phillips, Ernest	Pte	38104	Ombersley	20	kia	Péronne Road Cem
	Phipps, John James	Pte	45017	Birmingham	19	kia	Vis-en-Artois Memorial
	Spicer, Ernest Albert	Sgt	10042	Wallingford	21	kia	Péronne Road Cem
	Turk, Edward John	Pte	48534	Bristol		kia	Péronne Road Cem
	Walters, Ralph Richard	L/Cpl	220777	Balsall Heath		kia	Péronne Road Cem
	Warnock, Garvin	Pte	33715	Lanark	22	kia	Péronne Road Cem
	Whitehouse, Walter William	Pte	36762	West Bromwich		kia	Péronne Road Cem
	Wilkinson, Fred	Pte	39005	Tottingdon	22	kia	Péronne Road Cem
	Williams, Arthur Samuel	Pte	38046	Birmingham		dow	Daours Comm Cem Ext
27/08/18	Allen, William David	Pte	22328	Tilehurst		kia	Daours Comm Cem Ext
	Gamblin, Ernest	Pte	48717	Curland	19	dow	Daours Comm Cem Ext
	Martindale, George	L/Cpl	18303	Willesden	21	dow	Daours Comm Cem Ext
28/08/18	Clapp, John	Pte	45030	Silverton	19	dow	Daours Comm Cem Ext
	Tracy, Frank Eugene	L/Cpl	16549		21	dow	Daours Comm Cem Ext
29/08/18	Edwards, William Alfred	Pte	201599	Henley		dow	Daours Comm Cem Ext
01/09/18	Ashby, William Jennings	Pte	36233			dow	St Sever Cem Ext
02/09/18	Chapman, Leonard	2/Lieut			21	dow	St Sever Cem
06/09/18	Neal, Charles	Pte	33683	Sherston	32	dow	Dernancourt Comm Cem Ext
08/09/18	Street, Ernest	L/Cpl	39002	Burbage	27	dow	Abbeville Communal Cem Ext
09/09/18	Ball, Joseph Leslie	Pte	48633	Birmingham	19	dow	Varennes Mil Cem
10/09/18	Neal, Daniel Wiblet	Pte	45029	Churston		dow	Holy Cross Churchyard
11/09/18	Stanham, William Henry	L/Cpl	11234	Stanstead	23	died	Cologne Southern Cem
12/09/18	Cockle, Edward	Pte	45833	Leytonstone		kia	Epéhy Wood Farm Cem
14/09/18	Wollaston, George Edward	L/Cpl	11056	St Pancras	34	dow	Péronne Comm Cem Ext
18/09/18	Hambling, George Benjamin	Pte	45773	Reading	35	dow	Epéhy Wood Farm Cem
	Mercer, Wilfred	Pte	42937	Oldbury	20	kia	Epéhy Wood Farm Cem
	North, Arthur Allen	Pte	43082	Maidenhead	32	kia	Epéhy Wood Farm Cem
	Sampson, Harold Stanley	Pte	45775	Cronwood	23	kia	Epéhy Wood Farm Cem
	Smith, Benjamin	Pte	42958	Old Hill	20	kia	Epéhy Wood Farm Cem

Date	Name	Rank	Number	Birthplace	Age	Event	Cemetery name
19/09/18	Harding, Ernest Arthur	Pte	45800	Maidenhead		kia	Epéhy Wood Farm Cem
	Huckfield, Charles Hazlewood	Pte	42974	Oldbury	23	kia	Epéhy Wood Farm Cem
	Hussey, Leonard Thomas	Pte	48652	Stratton	19	kia	Epéhy Wood Farm Cem
	Nagel, Thomas Henry	Pte	39014	Snittisham	26	kia	Vis-en-Artois Memorial
	Preston, George	Pte	45092	Jersey CI		kia	Vis-en-Artois Memorial
	Smith, Wilfred Ernest	Pte	42910	Cradley	26	kia	Epéhy Wood Farm Cem
	Tebboth, William Henry	Pte	43564	Shenley	30	kia	Vis-en-Artois Memorial
	Webb, William	Pte	39028	Pontypridd		kia	Vis-en-Artois Memorial
20/09/18	Hatcher, Percy Charles	Pte	23612	Longstock	24	dow	Péronne Comm Cem Ext
21/09/18	Bedwood, Albert	Pte	48683	Birmingham		kia	Vis-en-Artois Memorial
	Edmonds, Frederick	Sgt	6190	Newington		kia	Vis-en-Artois Memorial
	Gould, James William	L/Cpl	9515	Shadwell		kia	Epéhy Wood Farm Cem
	Palmer, Wilfred	Pte	45782	Wroxton		dow	No entry in CWGC records
	Symes, Harold	Pte	220003	Stockport	25	kia	Vis-en-Artois Memorial
22/09/18	Cotterill, Walter	Pte	42913	Kettlebrook	27	kia	Epéhy Wood Farm Cem
	Davis, John Charles	L/Cpl	41624	Wolverhampton	20	kia	Vis-en-Artois Memorial
	Hands, Thomas William	Pte	33769	Manchester		kia	Péronne Comm Cem Ext
	Lloyd, Arthur	Pte	42237	Bewdley		kia	Epéhy Wood Farm Cem
	Pike, Charles Henry	Pte	203759	Exmouth	31	kia	Epéhy Wood Farm Cem
	Sionville, John Francis	Pte	203390	Jersey CI		kia	Vis-en-Artois Memorial
	Wagstaff, Percy James	Pte	45661	Birmingham	32	kia	Unicorn Cem
	Werrell, Charles	Pte	220286	Aylesbury	20	kia	Vis-en-Artois Memorial
23/09/18	Cahill, Charles Edward	Pte	45085	Devonport		kia	Péronne Comm Cem Ext
	Woolley, Frederick George	Pte	220783	Maidstone	36	died	Boisguillaume Comm Cem Ext
24/09/18	Goodchild, Owen Harold	L/Cpl	220523	Kimblewick		dow	Doingt Comm Cem Ext
25/09/18	Prickett, Arthur	Pte	203492	Reading	20	dow	Ste Marie Cem
26/09/18	Blight, Thomas Henry	Pte	48685	St Just		kia	Vis-en-Artois Memorial
	Bond, Ernest Frederick	2/Lieut			21	kia	Epéhy Wood Farm Cem
	Cookson, George Henry	Pte	42235	Amblecote	21	kia	Vis-en-Artois Memorial
	Drew, Ralph Treherne	Pte	48705	Bullo	19	kia	Vis-en-Artois Memorial
	Ellis, William	Pte	42936	Birmingham		kia	Vis-en-Artois Memorial
	Higgs, Stanger	Cpl	48569	Transvaal	19	dow	Doingt Comm Cem Ext
	Robinson, Alfred George	Pte	42895	Birmingham		kia	Vis-en-Artois Memorial
	Rogers, Harry	Pte	42929	Birmingham		kia	Villers Hill Brit Cem
	Williams, James	Pte	45835	Conway	28	kia	Villers Hill Brit Cem
27/09/18	Baxter, Frank	Pte	43984	Wolstanton		kia	Vis-en-Artois Memorial
	Ford, John Dewhurst	Pte	38407	St Lukes Lancs	35	dow	Le Cateau Mil Cem
	Forest, John	Pte	48708	Burford		kia	Vis-en-Artois Memorial
	Franklin, Frederick George	Pte	45143	Coombe	18	dow	Vis-en-Artois Memorial
	Griffiths, Ernest	Pte	42909	Wolverhampton	24	dow	Fontaine-au-Pire Comm Cem
	Ison, Francis Joseph	Pte	43083	Wimbledon	19	kia	Villers Hill Brit Cem
	Lawrence, Albert Dudley	Cpl	220713	London		kia	Villers Hill Brit Cem
	Reed, Albert Sorrel	Pte	36441		35	kia	Villers Hill Brit Cem
	Rushen, Walter William	Pte	39018	Heybridge	23	kia	Vis-en-Artois Memorial
28/09/18	Newman, William Henry	Pte	43077	Long Ditton	23	dow	Doingt Comm Cem Ext
29/09/18	Robinson, Wallace	Pte	42845	Denton	28	kia	Vis-en-Artois Memorial
02/10/18	Britton(or Britten), W E	Pte	220521	Lillingston Lovell	23	dow	Doingt Comm Cem Ext
03/10/18	Buckingham, William Albert	2/Lieut			31	dow	St Sever Cem Ext
05/10/18	Williams, John	Cpl	45770	Ottershaw	22	dow	St Sever Cem Ext
13/10/18	Digby, William Charles	Pte	45830	Hampton	26	kia	Point-du-Jour Mil Cem
14/10/18	Ash, Albert Edward	Pte	43781	Luton, Kent		kia	Liévin Comm Cem Ext
	Dugmore, Samuel Gregory	L/Sgt	227039	Birmingham	21	kia	Point-du-Jour Mil Cem
	Gane, Charles	Pte	48614	Evercreech	19	kia	Liévin Comm Cem Ext
	Green, Edward George	Pte	45050	Lowestoft	35	kia	Vis-en-Artois Memorial
	Merrick, James	Pte	45047		19	dow	Stourbridge Cem
	Upright, James Cobden	Pte	48615	Exeter	19	kia	Liévin Comm Cem Ext
	White, George Alexander	Pte	202939	Belgaum India	29	kia	Liévin Comm Cem Ext

Date	Name	Rank	Number	Birthplace	Age	Event	Cemetery name
15/10/18	Brennan, John Francis	Pte	42985	Coventry	19	dow	Houchin Brit Cem
	Buckland, Thomas Frank	Pte	201435	Windsor	22	kia	Orchard Dump Cem
	Moore, Frederick George	Pte	43406	Birmingham		kia	Orchard Dump Cem
	Nicoll, Harold Sidney	L/Cpl	220531		23	kia	Orchard Dump Cem
	Parsons, Nathaniel	Pte	48581	St Austell	19	kia	Point-du-Jour Mil Cem
	Simmonds, William	Pte	42903	Birmingham		kia	Vis-en-Artois Memorial
	Varney, William	Pte	9252	Stanford	25	dow	Houchin Brit Cem
16/10/18	Hayfield, George Harry	Pte	54151	Smethwick	19	dow	Houchin Brit Cem
	Hunt, Thomas Albert	Pte	43072	Redditch		kia	Vis-en-Artois Memorial
	Sydenham, Francis Victor	Pte	38611	Skilgate	20	kia	Dourges Comm Cem
	Vernon, Alfred	Pte	39004	Tarporley		dow	Houchin Brit Cem
17/10/18	Gatfield, Alfred	Pte	19411		34	died	Teddington Cem
18/10/18	Morris, Percival James	L/Cpl	45806	Stubbington		dow	Houchin Brit Cem
21/10/18	Southgate, Ernest Albert	Pte	43746	Ipswich		died	Hautmont Comm Cem
23/10/18	Werrell, Thomas	Pte	10883	Slough		died	Cologne Southern Cem
26/10/18	Wright, William Absalom	Pte	42833	Worcester	21	dow	Terlincthun Brit Cem
27/10/18	Hunt, Charles Gordon	Pte	44510	Worcester	26	dow	Terlincthun Brit Cem
28/10/18	Haynes, John	Pte	48722	Bromyard	19	dow	Douai Brit Cem
	Mumford, Ernest	Pte	16965	Hackney		dow	Niederzwehren Cem
29/10/18	Froggatte, George	Pte	16301	Hyde		dow	Terlincthun Brit Cem
	Mallam, Clifford Angus	Capt			28	dow	Douai Brit Cem
	Welch, Richard Ernest	Pte	45788	Hendon		died	Jeumont Comm Cem
31/10/18	Smith, George William	Pte	43093	Coventry	19	dow	Terlincthun Brit Cem
02/11/18	Baston, John	Pte	45803	Standlake		died	Hautmont Comm Cem
03/11/18	Bushell, John Bates	Pte	27115	Theale	33	died	St Sever Cem Ext
05/11/18	Ellis, Albert James	Sgt	10702	Bermondsey	23	died	Étaples Mil Cem
06/11/18	Galpin, Charles	Pte	10422	Banbury		died	Étaples Mil Cem
07/11/18	Lee, Gilbert	Pte	29583	High Wycombe		died	St Sever Cem Ext
12/11/18	Clarke, Vesey Douglas	Pte	48600	Milton Ernest	19	dow	Abbeville Communal Cem Ext
	Orrin, William John	2/Lieut			32	died	Ste Marie Cem Vieux Conde
15/11/18	Campbell, G E	Pte	45811		23	died	Étaples Mil Cem
17/11/18	Matthews, Edward John	Pte	30104	Bedminster	22	dow	Terlincthun Brit Cem
	Scott, Henry	Pte	45082		19	died	Terlincthun Brit Cem

6th Battalion

Date	Name	Rank	Number	Birthplace	Age	Event	Cemetery name
22/01/18	Osborne, Edward	Pte	25863	Tilehurst		died	Mendinghem Brit Cem
11/02/18	Rose, Charles Frederick	Pte	31646	High Wycombe	31	dow	High Wyc Churchyard
01/10/18	Hankins, John Frederick	Sgt	10134	Wantage		died	
18/11/18	Robinson, William R H	Pte	32165		24	died	Solesmes Brit Cem

Note: Although the 6th Battalion saw no action during 1918, and was disbanded in February, these men from the battalion were listed as dying during 1918, presumably from wounds during earlier actions.

8th Battalion

Date	Name	Rank	Number	Birthplace	Age	Event	Cemetery name
27/02/18	Bentley, Joseph	Pte	37194	Hadfield		kia	Grand Seraucourt Brit Cem
	Cutton, Robert Cecil	Pte	14911	Burton		dow	Grand Seraucourt Brit Cem
	Woodall, Norman	Pte	37157	Liverpool	29	kia	Thiepval Memorial
28/02/18	Spencer, Thomas	Pte	220164	Birmingham		dow	Grand Seraucourt Brit Cem
	Stilton, Frederick	Pte	37797	Aylesbury	28	dow	Montescourt-Lizerolles Cem
	Swallow, James	Pte	14876	Oldbury	35	dow	Grand Seraucourt Brit Cem
01/03/18	Hughes, Edward	A/CSM	15609	Birmingham	32	kia	Thiepval Memorial
	Pye, Henry	Sgt	37031	Walton		kia	Thiepval Memorial
09/03/18	Knight, David	Pte	37113	Runcorn	27	dow	Grand Seraucourt Brit Cem
18/03/18	Saunders, William Henry	Pte	220101		34	kia	Grand Seraucourt Brit Cem
20/03/18	Woodley, Walter	L/Cpl	17842	Mortimer		kia	Thiepval Memorial
21/03/18	Bloyce, William Henry	Pte	27170	Chislehurst	35	kia	Pozières Memorial
	Cartwright, Hartley	Pte	36638	Lye	31	kia	Pozières Memorial
	Chamberlain, Charles Alfred	Pte	13185	Buscot	32	kia	Pozières Memorial
	Chapman, Kenneth	Pte	37471	Northampton	22	kia	Pozières Memorial
	Clark, Frederick Percy	Pte	37322	Horton	24	kia	Pozières Memorial
	Clarke, John	L/Cpl	37074	Leigh		kia	Pozières Memorial
	Cooper, Percy George	Pte	36637	Lechlade	27	kia	Pozières Memorial
	Crocker, William	L/Cpl	18641	Reading	19	kia	Pozières Memorial
	Dennehy, Patrick James	L/Cpl	18274	Tullamore	25	kia	Pozières Memorial
	Dredge, Charles	Pte	34772	Reading		kia	Pozières Memorial
	Evans, William Brown	Pte	37162		22	kia	Pozières Memorial
	Farr, Frederick William	Pte	37896	Hereford	19	kia	Pozières Memorial
	Fleming, Richard	Pte	37089	Manchester		kia	Pozières Memorial
	Gordon, John Cameron	2/Lieut			27	kia	Pozières Memorial
	Harvey, Alfred James	L/Cpl	37809	Henley	19	kia	Pozières Memorial
	Harvey, Stanley Alfred George	Lieut			24	kia	Pozières Memorial
	Hawkins, William Reginald	Pte	25132	Abingdon		kia	Pozières Memorial
	Herbert, Harry	Pte	36219	Bristol		kia	Pozières Memorial
	Howell, Ernest William	Pte	30881	Gloucester	30	kia	Pozières Memorial
	Hughes, William Henry	Pte	37103	Upton	27	kia	Pozières Memorial
	Johnson, Thomas William	L/Cpl	34077	Easthampstead		kia	Pozières Memorial
	King, Eric George	2/Lieut			31	kia	Pozières Memorial
	King, Herbert Charles	Pte	26564	Gt Coxwell	22	kia	Pozières Memorial
	Kitson, Herbert	L/Cpl	18609	Poplar		kia	Pozières Memorial
	Kneller, Henry Thomas	Pte	18448	Poplar		kia	Plaine Fr Nat Cem
	Lowrey, Charles	Pte	14379	Limerick	25	kia	Pozières Memorial
	Painter, Albert	Pte	18034	Burfield		kia	Pozières Memorial
	Palmer, Archibald John	Pte	16381	Marsh Benham	32	kia	Pozières Memorial
	Perry, Richard Alexander	Pte	230131	Birmingham		kia	Pozières Memorial
	Pizzey, Edward	Pte	20170	Reading		kia	Pozières Memorial
	Pocock, Joseph	Pte	201028	Thatcham		kia	Pozières Memorial
	Prescott, John	Pte	37134	Runcorn	21	kia	Pozières Memorial
	Ransom, Harry Arthur	Pte	33116	Petersfield		kia	Pozières Memorial
	Simmonds, Arthur	Pte	36833	Manchester		kia	Pozières Memorial
	Smith, Herbert	Pte	37781	Longwick		kia	Pozières Memorial
	Smith, James	Sgt	37043		22	kia	Pozières Memorial
	Sumpster, Frank Mariner	Lieut			29	kia	Pozières Memorial
	Tosetti, Douglas	Major			40	kia	Pozières Memorial
	Venn, Tom	Pte	21837	Wootton under Edge		kia	Pozières Memorial
	Willerton, Harry	Pte	36943	Gainsborough		kia	Pozières Memorial
	Williams, Norman	Lieut			22	kia	Pozières Memorial
	Willis, Robert Edwin	Pte	19126	Birmingham	21	dow	Pozières Memorial
23/03/18	Hughes, Charles Edward	Pte	13580	Bray		dow	Noyon New Brit Cem
	Stant, Frank	L/Cpl	36977	Winsford	21	kia	Chauny Comm Cem Brit Ext

Date	Name	Rank	Number	Birthplace	Age	Event	Cemetery name
23/03/18	Willoughby, Joseph	Sgt	15252	Binfield	26	dow	Séry-les-Mézières Comm Cem
	Young, John Thomas	Pte	37057		31	kia	Pozières Memorial
25/03/18	Bailey, Henry Frederick	Pte	15050	Bath		kia	Pozières Memorial
26/03/18	Woodward, Herbert George	Pte	34130	Kidlington	19	dow	Ribemont Comm Cem Ext
27/03/18	Parker, Arthur Charles	Pte	32897	Kidmore End		died	St Sever Cem Ext
29/03/18	Burnard, James	Pte	37787	High Wycombe	33	dow	Guise Fr Nat Cem
31/03/18	Clarke, Harold Frank	Pte	39380	Wellington		kia	Pozières Memorial
	Grange, William Henry	Pte	18415	High Wycombe		kia	Pozières Memorial
	Lewendon, Frederick Ernest	Pte	21766	Reading	26	kia	Pozières Memorial
	Warr, William Basil	Pte	36795	Warwick		kia	Pozières Memorial
01/04/18	Knight, Edward	Pte	21597	Bray	30	dow	St Sever Cem Ext
	Seabrook, William John	Pte	17274	Lambeth	19	dow	Namps-au-Val Brit Cem
03/04/18	Breadmore, William George	Pte	20182	Brightwalton	26	dow	Hautmont Comm Cem
	Gosbee, Levi	Cpl	17270	Blackfriars		kia	Maroc Brit Cem
04/04/18	Attwood, William John	Pte	34372	Birmingham		kia	Pozières Memorial
	Cook, George Alexander	Pte	17719	Oxford		kia	Pozières Memorial
	Crook, Bert	Pte	12776	Salisbury	20	kia	Pozières Memorial
	Dewing, Robert Edward	Lt/Col			30	kia	Pozières Memorial
	Longhurst, Arthur	Pte	22248	Ascot	21	kia	Pozières Memorial
	Sarchet, Hugh le Gallienne	Capt				kia	Pozières Memorial
	Wale, Edmund Joseph	L/Cpl	30871	Carrickfergus		dow	Pozières Memorial
06/04/18	Caden, Harry	Pte	15011	Birmingham		dow	Namps-au-Val Brit Cem
07/04/18	Giddings, Stanley N G	Sgt	14341	Devizes	23	dow	Picquigny Brit Cem
08/04/18	Slater, Cyril George	Pte	44979	Rugby	19	kia	Vis-en-Artois Memorial
09/04/18	Long, John	Pte	21591	Warfield	20	kia	Boves East Comm Cem
	White, Sidney Llewellyn	Pte	220185	East Langton		kia	Boves East Comm Cem
	Wogan, William Patrick	Pte	17967	Shoreditch	40	kia	Boves East Comm Cem
15/04/18	Irving, James	Pte	21583	Birmingham	21	dow	Tourgeville Mil Cem
19/04/18	Bayliss, Harry	Pte	203420	Kidderminster	43	dow	Niederzwehren Cem
23/04/18	Duffin, William	Pte	32855	Mortimer	33	died	St Mary's Churchyard
	Matthews, Elijah James	Pte	25078	Bristol		died	Grand Seraucourt Brit Cem
24/04/18	Grady, Sidney	Pte	220168	Birmingham		kia	Vis-en-Artois Memorial
25/04/18	Long, James	Sgt	36722	Kidderminster	30	dow	Kidderminster Cem
01/05/18	Davis, Gilbert Charles	Pte	39458	Naunton		died	Ribemont Comm Cem Ext
11/05/18	Handley, George	A/Cpl	21016	Birmingham	34	dow	St Sever Cem Ext
	Hill, Arthur George	Pte	41604	Birmingham		kia	Senlis Comm Cem Ext
	Samways, William James	Pte	43672	Chard	22	kia	Senlis Comm Cem Ext
12/05/18	Lombard, Harry	Pte	44662	Coventry	19	kia	Dernancourt Comm Cem Ext
	Murphy, Charles	L/Cpl	14146	Westminster		kia	Dernancourt Comm Cem Ext
14/05/18	Rawlings, Daniel William	Pte	45134	Warwick	19	dow	Pernois Brit Cem
15/05/18	Harding, William Thomas	Pte	44583	Aylesbury	19	dow	Pernois Brit Cem
19/05/18	Gibbons, Thomas John	Pte	14641	Birmingham		died	Annois Comm Cem
20/05/18	Pearce, David Charles	Pte	16470	Newbury		died	Grand Seraucourt Brit Cem
23/05/18	Howlett, Harold George	Pte	44661	Shanklin IOW	19	kia	Ribemont Comm Cem Ext
25/05/18	Feakes, William Alfred	Pte	36645	Dudley	34	died	Annois Comm Cem
30/05/18	Stuckey, William Edward	Pte	14452	Sunningdale	21	died	Annois Comm Cem
02/06/18	Robinson, Charles Telford	Pte	44746	Edmonton	18	kia	Ribemont Comm Cem Ext
04/06/18	Fryer, Albert Robert	Pte	19928	Reading	24	kia	Ribemont Comm Cem Ext
	George, John Richard	Pte	21865	Bristol	25	kia	Ribemont Comm Cem Ext
06/06/18	Andrews, Frederick	Pte	36799	Redditch		died	Niederzwehren Cem
	Benfield, Walter John	Pte	13207	Ledwell	26	died	St Sever Cem Ext
13/06/18	Evitts, Joseph	Pte	14821	Oldbury	33	dow	Calais Southern Cem
21/06/18	Fullbrook, Robert George	Pte	34771	Spencers Wood		died	Belgrade Comm Cem, Namur
23/06/18	Rowland, George Charles	L/Sgt	15625	Childrey		kia	Pozières Memorial
	Stone, George Arthur	L/Cpl	202538	Braintree		died	Queens Road Cem
29/06/18	Alcock, Alfred Charles	Pte	220141	Leamington	20	died	Hautmont Comm Cem
	Freeman, Joseph Sidney	Pte	35127	Wallingford	35	died	Berlin South Western Cem

Appendix V

Date	Name	Rank	Number	Birthplace	Age	Event	Cemetery name
01/07/18	Cull, Sidney Edward	Pte	220187	Christchurch	38	died	Berlin South Western Cem
	Patey, William Charles	Pte	44736	Portsmouth	19	kia	Ribemont Comm Cem Ext
02/07/18	Garner, James Arthur	L/Cpl	12710	Lambeth		died	No entry in CWGC records
07/07/18	Cockram, William John	Pte	44993	Birmingham	19	kia	Ribemont Comm Cem Ext
	Fripps, Charles	Pte	45007	Marylebone	19	kia	Ribemont Comm Cem Ext
	House, Harold	Pte	45060	Kingsomborne	19	dow	Pernois Brit Cem
10/07/18	Wheeler, Bertie James	Pte	15044	Appleford		died	Sedan (St Charles) Cem
20/07/18	Walker, Frederick Charles	Pte	36983	Northwich	21	kia	Cronenbourg Fr Nat Cem
27/07/18	Hitchman, Alfred	Pte	45629	Worcester		kia	Caterpillar Valley Cem
29/07/18	Sleeman, Harold John	Pte	36699	Boynton	22	died	Berlin South Western Cem
08/08/18	Andrews, William George	Pte	210017		21	kia	Vis-en-Artois Memorial
	Barker, Thomas Frederick	Pte	45510	Binfield		kia	Vis-en-Artois Memorial
	Bendle, James Alfred	Pte	44502	Barnstaple		kia	Beacon Cem
	Bray, Aubrey Mellish	Lieut		Sunderland	24	dow	Vignacourt Brit Cem
	Collett, Frederick Yeeles	Pte	45529	Bath	18	kia	Vis-en-Artois Memorial
	Crang, George Joseph	Pte	18519	Paddington	23	kia	Beacon Cem
	Cross, William Henry	Pte	45520	Plymouth	18	kia	Beacon Cem
	Darvarashvili, Isaac	Pte	41649	Palestine	25	kia	Beacon Cem
	Edge, Richard	Pte	201944	York	35	kia	Beacon Cem
	Ewens, Mark	Pte	203710	Crewkerne	28	kia	Beacon Cem
	Griffiths, Albert Henry	Pte	21885	Barton Hill	26	kia	Vis-en-Artois Memorial
	Hamblett, Melville Augustus	Pte	44612	Gloucester	19	kia	Vis-en-Artois Memorial
	Hathaway, Walter Henry	Pte	44550	Stroud		kia	Beacon Cem
	Holloway, Frederick	Pte	44698			kia	Vis-en-Artois Memorial
	Hudson, Howard	Pte	220738	Handsworth	18	kia	Vis-en-Artois Memorial
	Ingram, John Henry	Pte	35434	Bethnal Grn		kia	Beacon Cem
	James, Wilfred	Pte	44703	Holmer Grn		kia	Beacon Cem
	Keynton, William John	Pte	44579	Wootton under Edge	19	kia	Vis-en-Artois Memorial
	Layden, Frank	Pte	45073	Cleckheaton	20	kia	Vis-en-Artois Memorial
	Livesley, Charles Samuel	Pte	9233	Birmingham		kia	Vis-en-Artois Memorial
	Lound, Walter Edward	Pte	44771	Wileford		kia	Vis-en-Artois Memorial
	Moss, Charles William	2/Lieut			30	kia	Beacon Cem
	Nichols, John	Pte	42377	Birmingham		kia	Albert Communal Cem Ext
	Norman, Francis Herbert	Pte	44630	Bristol	19	kia	Beacon Cem
	Ostridge, Charles Henry	Cpl	31410	Reading	26	kia	Beacon Cem
	Petley, Lionel	Pte	36747	Cowes IoW	24	kia	Beacon Cem
	Pullman, Albert	Pte	42211	Portsmouth	19	kia	Beacon Cem
	Roberts, Ewart James	Pte	45540	Exeter	19	kia	Beacon Cem
	Roche, Frederick	Pte	220142	Birmingham	23	kia	Vis-en-Artois Memorial
	Sharman, George William	Pte	203301	Birmingham		kia	Beacon Cem
	Sim, Ronald James	Pte	200118	Clapham	23	kia	Villers-Bretonneux Mil Cem
	Stafford, George William	Pte	44536	Bedminster		kia	Beacon Cem
	Teece, George Henry	Pte	43671	Hanley	25	kia	Vis-en-Artois Memorial
	Walker, Roland	Pte	13108	Stanstead Abbot	24	kia	Vis-en-Artois Memorial
	Weait, John Holder	L/Cpl	31412	Reading	22	kia	Vis-en-Artois Memorial
	Wilkinson, Frank	Pte	20053	Lambeth		kia	Beacon Cem
	Woodey, Albert George	L/Cpl	43540	Bristol		kia	Péronne Comm Cem Ext
	Woodward, John	Pte	44973	Kingswinford		kia	Beacon Cem
	Wyatt, John Thomas	L/Sgt	36724	Birmingham		kia	Beacon Cem
09/08/18	Charlett, George	Pte	37078	Chester	26	dow	Pernois Brit Cem
	Veare, David	Pte	44980	Gloucester	19	dow	Pernois Brit Cem
10/08/18	Stringer, Reginald John	CSM	9135	Oxford	27	dow	Pernois Brit Cem
12/08/18	Roberts, Frederick John	Pte	45535	Portland	18	dow	St Sever Cem Ext
18/08/18	Emmett, Albert Edward	Pte	19664	Reading	24	kia	Vis-en-Artois Memorial
22/08/18	Leech, Sidney William	Cpl	14898	Smethwick	22	dow	Birmingham (Lodge Hill) Cem
23/08/18	Edwards, Joseph	Pte	220210	Wroughton	24	kia	Albert Communal Cem Ext
	Porter, William Henry George	Pte	45621	Bristol	25	kia	Albert Communal Cem Ext

Date	Name	Rank	Number	Birthplace	Age	Event	Cemetery name
23/08/18	Yellan, Francis William	Pte	32872	Reading	20	kia	Albert Communal Cem Ext
24/08/18	Butler, Ernest	Pte	45566	Gt Marlow		kia	Vis-en-Artois Memorial
	Guy, Reginald Churchill	2/Lieut				kia	Dernancourt Comm Cem Ext
	Lewis, Reginald Wolstan	Pte	45072	Cardiff	18	kia	Bapaume Post Mil Cem
	Moore, Philip Archibald T	Pte	43701	Hastings	28	dow	Daours Comm Cem Ext
	Perks, Edwin Sidney.	Pte	44967	Hawkesbury		kia	Bapaume Post Mil Cem
	Stanley, William Henry	Pte	45583	Bodicote		kia	Vis-en-Artois Memorial
	Upfield, Stanley George	Pte	44651	Gosport	19	kia	Vis-en-Artois Memorial
25/08/18	Brooks, Charles	Pte	45570	Woodstock	30	dow	Daours Comm Cem Ext
26/08/18	Dorrell, Arthur James	Pte	220505		20	dow	Daours Comm Cem Ext
	Eustace, William	Pte	19992	Wantage	20	died	Hautmont Comm Cem
27/08/18	Adams, William George	Pte	34648	Ilminster		kia	Vis-en-Artois Memorial
	Backhurst, Herbert James	Pte	45506	Hartley Wintney		kia	Bernafay Wood Brit Cem
	Bardell, Harry Henry	Pte	44576	Birmingham		kia	Vis-en-Artois Memorial
	Batts, John	Pte	37897	Witney	20	kia	Albert Communal Cem Ext
	Beesley, Harry James	Pte	45515	Clewer	18	kia	Vis-en-Artois Memorial
	Brown, Stanley Newman	2/Lieut			25	kia	Longueval Road Cem
	Buckley, George William	2/Lieut			31	kia	Bécourt Military Cem
	Burgess, James	Pte	220016	Alsager	26	kia	Vis-en-Artois Memorial
	Collins, Albert	Pte	45519	Reading	18	kia	Vis-en-Artois Memorial
	Colwell, Dennis	Pte	44507	Stanton St John	19	kia	Caterpillar Valley Cem
	Delamare, George Herbert	Pte	18122	Blackwall	20	kia	Bouzincourt Comm Cem Ext
	Dibley, Charles	Pte	201693	Reading		kia	Bernafay Wood Brit Cem
	Dines, Edward Arthur	Pte	43649	Ipswich	28	kia	Bernafay Wood Brit Cem
	Gilbert, Charles Stephen	Pte	43682	Islington	27	kia	Bernafay Wood Brit Cem
	Herbert, Frank	Pte	43667	Odiham	24	kia	Bernafay Wood Brit Cem
	Hopwood, Frederick W	2/Lieut				kia	Quarry Cem
	Jackson, Edward William	Pte	45654	Norwich	26	kia	Caterpillar Valley Cem
	Jones, Albert	Pte	38775	Birmingham		kia	Longueval Road Cem
	Kirkaldie, Ethelbert	Pte	43687	Deal	25	kia	Vis-en-Artois Memorial
	Lewis, Stanley William	Pte	44770	Gloucester		kia	Caterpillar Valley Cem
	Lovegrove, Harry	Pte	27252	Birmingham	24	kia	Bouzincourt Comm Cem Ext
	Moore, Harry	Pte	220444	Tisbury	24	kia	Bernafay Wood Brit Cem
	Norris, Ernest	Pte	31333	Easthampstead	20	kia	Bernafay Wood Brit Cem
	Northover, Frederick Charles	Pte	44916	Murtonstone	19	kia	Bernafay Wood Brit Cem
	Parsons, Joseph	Pte	44733	Cradley		kia	Bernafay Wood Brit Cem
	Rogers, James Robert	Pte	45589	Bristol	28	kia	Vis-en-Artois Memorial
	Salter, Albert George	Pte	44643	Hemyock	19	kia	Delville Wood Cem
	Seear, Sidney Walter	Pte	36971	Poplar	23	kia	Bernafay Wood Brit Cem
	Smith, Sidney	Pte	33053	Henley		kia	Caterpillar Valley Cem
	Stacey, Henry John	Pte	28773	Reading	20	kia	Caterpillar Valley Cem
	Steward, Arthur Thomas	Pte	45643	Withal	25	kia	Bernafay Wood Brit Cem
	Taber, William	L/Cpl	16154	Bordon	28	kia	Bernafay Wood Brit Cem
	Talbot, William Allen	Pte	220742	West Bromwich		kia	Bécourt Military Cem
	Townsend, Albert	Pte	30851	London	21	kia	Bernafay Wood Brit Cem
	Trinder, Claude Vincent	Pte	35357	Chadlington	19	kia	Longueval Road Cem
	Webb, Richard	CSM	27221	Cumnor	34	kia	Bernafay Wood Brit Cem
	Welch, Thomas	Pte	43681	Crewe	28	kia	Albert Communal Cem Ext
	White, Arthur Edward	Pte	9282	Cookham		kia	Longueval Road Cem
	Wilde, Ernest William	Pte	45597	Selly Oak		kia	Bernafay Wood Brit Cem
	Willmott, Henry George	Pte	44664	Gosport	19	kia	Longueval Road Cem
	Wills, William Charles	Pte	45623	Hammersmith		dow	Daours Comm Cem Ext
	Wort, Sidney	L/Cpl	203751	Romsey		kia	Bernafay Wood Brit Cem
28/08/18	Birch, Samuel Bernard	Cpl	203824	Walsall		kia	Vis-en-Artois Memorial
	Butler, Albert	L/Cpl	201730	Fareham	26	kia	Lonsdale Cem
	Hammond, Joseph	Pte	45126	Warwick	19	dow	Daours Comm Cem Ext
	Horne, Harold	Pte	45582	Maidstone	28	kia	Bernafay Wood Brit Cem

Appendix V

Date	Name	Rank	Number	Birthplace	Age	Event	Cemetery name
28/08/18	Lunnon, Herbert	Sgt	45640	Marlow	22	kia	Longueval Road Cem
	Rogers, Alfred John	Pte	45130		19	dow	Fienvillers Brit Cem
	Thomas, Sidney	L/Cpl	20122	Birmingham	27	kia	Vis-en-Artois Memorial
	Wassell, Samuel	Pte	44571	Lye	19	dow	Daours Comm Cem Ext
	Watts, Thomas Francis	Pte	45608	Twyford		dow	Daours Comm Cem Ext
	Wharf, Charles	Pte	36508	Balham		kia	Longueval Road Cem
29/08/18	Wheeler, Harry Cussell	L/Cpl	200855	Reading	22	dow	Ste Marie Cem
30/08/18	Lawrence, Robert French	Pte	41594	Bristol	19	dow	Daours Comm Cem Ext
	Walker, Percy Thomas	Pte	45501	Chilton	27	dow	Daours Comm Cem Ext
01/09/18	Clift, Edwin John	Pte	44976	Woodchester		dow	Heilly Station Cem
	Edmunds, Stanley	Sgt	36793	Halesowen	22	dow	Daours Comm Cem Ext
	Smith, Frank George	Cpl	11690	Abingdon	26	dow	Daours Comm Cem Ext
	Whiting, Frank	Pte	16647	Hungerford		dow	Boisguillaume Comm Cem Ext
02/09/18	Fothergill, Frederick	Pte	220117	Birmingham		kia	Vis-en-Artois Memorial
	Gould, Walter	Pte	44935	Loughborough	19	kia	Vis-en-Artois Memorial
	Payne, Thomas	Pte	43760	Christchurch	23	kia	Vis-en-Artois Memorial
	Watts, Stanley	Pte	38620	Odiham		kia	Vis-en-Artois Memorial
03/09/18	Baker, Frederick	Cpl	15587	Minster Lovell		kia	No entry in cwgc records
	Dodd, Redvers Kitchener	Pte	45879	Basingstoke		dow	Dernancourt Comm Cem Ext
	Matthews, Frank	Pte	220508		27	died	Vis-en-Artois Memorial
04/09/18	Jones, Thomas	Pte	45609	Maids Moreton	18	kia	Vis-en-Artois Memorial
	Wakefield, George Osborne	Pte	37789	West Wycombe	33	died	Niederzwehren Cem
	Ware, John	Pte	19984	Reading		died	Berlin South Western Cem
05/09/18	Shepherd, William	Pte	36457		29	dow	St Sever Cem Ext
06/09/18	Opie, Charles	Pte	45945	Rochdale	18	dow	Dernancourt Comm Cem Ext
07/09/18	Holloway, Percy George	Cpl	200459	Burghfield	24	dow	Daours Comm Cem Ext
	Sanders, William Honeyman	Pte	202048	Exeter	34	dow	Etretat Churchyard Ext
09/09/18	Baker, Frank Albert	L/Cpl	45504	Barford		kia	Ste Emilie Valley Cem
	Hollyman, Frank	Pte	39122	Dinton	19	dow	Ss Peter & Paul Churchyard
10/09/18	Russ, Walter Clement	Pte	44638	Birmingham	19	dow	Cologne Southern Cem
11/09/18	Prickett, Louis William	Pte	45648	Banbury		kia	St Sever Cem Ext
16/09/18	Anns, Henry	Pte	16388	East Hendred		died	Hautmont Comm Cem
17/09/18	Bennett, Samuel Richard	Pte	44681	St Columb, Cornwall		kia	Ste Emilie Valley Cem
	Green, Herbert John	Pte	43022	Frampton Cotterill	22	kia	Unicorn Cem
	Turner, Alfred Edgar	Pte	44941	Stanton StJohn	19	kia	Ste Emilie Valley Cem
19/09/18	Bayliss, Ernest Albert	Pte	45511	Weston		dow	Péronne Comm Cem Ext
	Clutson, Stanley	Pte	45522	Bristol	18	kia	Vis-en-Artois Memorial
	Cumbley, Reginald	2/Lieut			30	kia	Unicorn Cem
	Haynes, George	L/Cpl	45123	Trentham		kia	Unicorn Cem
	Mills, Reginald David	Pte	43007	Birmingham	21	kia	Vis-en-Artois Memorial
	Musselwhite, Albert George	Pte	45930	Downton	19	kia	Vis-en-Artois Memorial
	Nash, Alfred George	Pte	44966	Limpsfield	29	kia	Vis-en-Artois Memorial
	Nichols, Charles Henry	Pte	45940	Bristol	18	kia	Vis-en-Artois Memorial
	Taylor, Arthur Lionel	Pte	43699	Portsmouth	23	kia	Unicorn Cem
	Walter, Harold Burgoyne	A/Cpl	220735	Bristol		kia	Unicorn Cem
	Wassell, Thomas Henry	Pte	43344	Wallescote	20	kia	Vis-en-Artois Memorial
20/09/18	Barber, Stanley	Pte	38106	Bewdley		dow	Doingt Comm Cem Ext
	Bishop, William Frederick	Pte	35896	Worcester	23	kia	Vis-en-Artois Memorial
	Brombley, Owen	Pte	45838	Easthampstead		kia	Vis-en-Artois Memorial
	Butler, Robert William	L/Cpl	202477			kia	Vis-en-Artois Memorial
	Dell, George Abel	L/Cpl	201168	West Drayton	23	kia	Vis-en-Artois Memorial
	Gee, Robert	Pte	35510	Birmingham	21	kia	Unicorn Cem
	Harper, Harold Hubert	Pte	43250	Coventry	21	kia	Vis-en-Artois Memorial
	Henshaw, Arthur	Pte	37100	Northwich	21	kia	Vis-en-Artois Memorial
	Jones, Ernest Thomas	Pte	43723	Glasbury	29	kia	Vis-en-Artois Memorial
	Kempton, Roger	Pte	36371		24	kia	Vis-en-Artois Memorial
	Laight, Sidney	Pte	44719	Alcester	19	kia	Vis-en-Artois Memorial

Date	Name	Rank	Number	Birthplace	Age	Event	Cemetery name
20/09/18	Lees, Wallace	Pte	43339	Two Gates, Warks	23	kia	Vis-en-Artois Memorial
	Mace, James	Pte	43265	Newbury	19	kia	Vis-en-Artois Memorial
	Pearman, Edward Percy	Pte	44634	Sherfield	19	kia	Vis-en-Artois Memorial
	Penhale, Dennis Walter	Pte	44737	Christon	19	kia	Vis-en-Artois Memorial
	Pill, William Henry	Pte	37695	Shillingford		kia	Vis-en-Artois Memorial
	Risby, John	Pte	44640	Edge		kia	Vis-en-Artois Memorial
	Westbury, Norman	Pte	43347	Netherend		kia	Vis-en-Artois Memorial
21/09/18	Beecham, Jesse	Pte	44776	Leeds	36	kia	Vis-en-Artois Memorial
	Cottrell, Arthur	Pte	45878	Wokingham	19	kia	Vis-en-Artois Memorial
	Goddard, Ernest Herbert	Pte	43366	Coventry		kia	Unicorn Cem
	Holmes, George	Pte	202009	Andover		kia	Vis-en-Artois Memorial
	Parker, William	Pte	18152	Woodbram Walter		dow	Doingt Comm Cem Ext
	Plaster, Wilfred Gilbert	Pte	44773	Wood Grn		kia	Vis-en-Artois Memorial
22/09/18	Taylor, William Henry	Pte	202862		19	kia	Vis-en-Artois Memorial
23/09/18	Bennetton, Albert Thomas	Pte	44682	Godalming	19	kia	Vis-en-Artois Memorial
	Carrier, Jack James	L/Cpl	17496	Canning Town	21	dow	Doingt Comm Cem Ext
	Emmett, Austin	Pte	37687	Westbury		kia	Vis-en-Artois Memorial
	Hull, Frank	L/Cpl	44607	Hurst		kia	Vis-en-Artois Memorial
	Jackson, George	Pte	45918	Halesowen		kia	No entry in CWGC records
	Smithers, Walter Malcome	Pte	45974	Newport IoW		kia	Vis-en-Artois Memorial
24/09/18	Edwards, Frank	Pte	43650	Weston Supermare	28	dow	Péronne Comm Cem Ext
	Jacobs, Edwin	Pte	43658	Brading IOW	23	dow	Doingt Comm Cem Ext
25/09/18	Liddiard, Reginald Francis	Pte	44620	Liddington	19	dow	Doingt Comm Cem Ext
	Millson, William	Pte	20128	Bradfield	27	died	Annois Comm Cem
29/09/18	Clarke, John Lionel	Pte	44596	Birmingham		died	Vis-en-Artois Memorial
	Grant, Ernest Clargo	Pte	45089	Reading	19	died	Le Cateau Mil Cem
06/10/18	Hall, Sidney Herbert	Pte	45014	Avington	19	died	Crossroads Cem
09/10/18	Glazier, Charles	Pte	43736	Wimbledon		dow	Grévillers Brit Cem
21/10/18	Bunce, Arthur John	Cpl	8072	Christchurch		dow	Reading Cem
22/10/18	Ball, Harry	Pte	44768	Leek	32	dow	Villers-Bretonneux Mil Cem
23/10/18	Allen, Alfred Gilbert	Pte	45498	Reading	18	kia	Vis-en-Artois Memorial
	Beaufoy, Arthur	CSM	14559	Coventry		kia	Le Cateau Mil Cem
	Blackburn, Norman H G	2/Lieut				kia	Highland Cem
	Cleaver, James	Pte	45873	Congerstone		kia	Le Cateau Mil Cem
	Dare, Gilbert Arthur	L/Cpl	44075	Marshfield	20	died	Villers-Bretonneux Mil Cem
	Fisher, Frank Richard	Pte	200191	Reading	30	kia	Highland Cem
	Gilbert, William	Pte	220449	London		kia	Highland Cem
	Goodyear, Hector Robert	Pte	45894	Callow End		kia	Highland Cem
	Hemmings, Ernest John	L/Cpl	41418	Abingdon	35	kia	Highland Cem
	Higham, Ernest Edward	Pte	45902	Nuneaton	18	kia	Le Cateau Mil Cem
	Howe, Sidney John	Pte	45908	Cullompton		kia	Le Cateau Mil Cem
	Keen, Frank	Pte	220276	Over Norton		kia	Highland Cem
	Kelynack, William Harry	Pte	44619	Paul, Cornwall	19	kia	Pommereuil Brit Cem
	Mullins, Alfred Ernest	Pte	45936	Birmingham	18	kia	Highland Cem
	Napper, Reginald Charlie	Pte	45943	Cannington Som		dow	Highland Cem
	Newman, Harry	Pte	45941	Ropley	18	kia	Vis-en-Artois Memorial
	Parker, Ralph Jones	Pte	45959	Wells	18	kia	Highland Cem
	Paul, Charles Henry	Pte	45947	Portsmouth	18	kia	Vis-en-Artois Memorial
	Stacey, Ernest	Pte	33927	Tilehurst		kia	Highland Cem
	Stevens, Harry	Pte	201761	Aylesbury		kia	Le Cateau Mil Cem
	Stew, Joseph	Pte	43258	Coleshill	29	kia	Highland Cem
	Tattam, Hayden Stewart	L/Cpl	37801	Drayton Parslow	26	kia	Highland Cem
	Treadwell, Alfred	Pte	12248	Winshill	23	dow	Prémont Brit Cem
	Tyrrell, Frederick Henry	Pte	37783	Curtlington	35	kia	Highland Cem
	White, Percival	Pte	43698	Somerton	32	kia	Le Cateau Mil Cem
24/10/18	Adelstone, Claude	Pte	42963	Birmingham	36	dow	Prémont Brit Cem
	Thomas, Alfred Charles	Pte	33282	Southampton		dow	St Sever Cem Ext

Appendix V

Date	Name	Rank	Number	Birthplace	Age	Event	Cemetery name
24/10/18	Tucker, Frederick George	Pte	202086	Draycott	28	died	Villers-Bretonneux Mil Cem
25/10/18	Herridge, Arthur	Pte	203953	Ascot		died	St Sever Cem Ext
26/10/18	Best, William James	Pte	45860	Kingsbury		kia	Preux-au-Bois Comm Cem
	Blakey, Thomas	Pte	44767	Gateshead	32	kia	Vis-en-Artois Memorial
	Bushby, Ernest	Pte	36251		27	kia	Romeries Comm Cem Ext
	Fox, William	Pte	45632	Brize Norton		kia	Vis-en-Artois Memorial
27/10/18	Harper, Frederick Charles	Pte	45135	Warwick	18	kia	Vis-en-Artois Memorial
	Mildren, James	Pte	45928	Penzance	18	kia	Vis-en-Artois Memorial
	Siviter, Braithet Eustace	Pte	45984	Hunnington	18	kia	Vis-en-Artois Memorial
28/10/18	Dawes, Sydney	Pte	39382	Southrop	32	died	St Sever Cem Ext
	Jones, John	Pte	43329	Birmingham	37	kia	Honnechy Brit Cem
29/10/18	Reed, Stanley	Pte	43716	Tynemouth		dow	St Sever Cem Ext
30/10/18	Munday, Cuthbert J	Pte	16452			died	St Michaels Churchyard
31/10/18	Robey, Frank Ernest	Pte	44939	Watchfield		dow	Awoingt British Cem
02/11/18	Bessant, Percival Frederick	Pte	45853	Cheddar	18	dow	St Sever Cem Ext
	Hinton, Walter Daniel	Pte	45063	St Pancras	19	kia	Honnechy Brit Cem
03/11/18	Sutton, Walter Ernest	Cpl	202956	Bedminster	33	died	Abbeville Communal Cem Ext
04/11/18	Barr, Benjamin	Pte	45840	Birmingham	18	kia	Vis-en-Artois Memorial
	Bond, Clifford	Pte	44680	N Newton		kia	Montay-Neuvilly Rd Cem
	Brittle, Archie Robert	Pte	45846	Birmingham		kia	Vis-en-Artois Memorial
	Easthope, Ernest	Pte	27381	Birmingham		kia	Vis-en-Artois Memorial
	Field, Leslie Jack	2/Lieut			23	kia	Montay-Neuvilly Rd Cem
	Hanmer, Sidney Arthur	Pte	220130	Birmingham	23	kia	Montay-Neuvilly Rd Cem
	Jones, Edward	Pte	43265	Birmingham	37	kia	Preux-au-Bois Comm Cem
	Latham, Herbert William	Pte	44622	Warwick		kia	Montay-Neuvilly Rd Cem
	Long, John	2/Lieut			23	kia	Preux-au-Bois Comm Cem
	Nichols, Ernest Leonard	Pte	43281	Plaistow	20	kia	Preux-au-Bois Comm Cem
	Roberts, Frederick Ernest	Pte	45962	Wimbourne		kia	Montay-Neuvilly Rd Cem
	Sharp, Charles Henry	Pte	44642	Birmingham	19	kia	Vis-en-Artois Memorial
	Bradford, William	Pte	10155	Islington		dow	Prémont Brit Cem
05/11/18	Carpenter, Harry	Pte	43721	Bishops Hull	22	died	Etretat Churchyard Ext
	Peters, Joseph Edward	Cpl	36687	Berrow		dow	St Sever Cem Ext
07/11/18	Caudrey, Frank Percy	Pte	45649	Wendover		died	Tourgéville Mil Cem
08/11/18	Douglas, Robert	Cpl	45612	Netherall		dow	Busigny Comm Cem Ext
12/11/18	Busby, Albert John	Pte	44947	Hatton	19	died	St Sever Cem Ext
	Smith, Christopher	L/Sgt	44670	Liverpool NSW		dow	Birmingham (Lodge Hill) Cem
02/12/18	Harrison, G	Sgt	36810			died	Niederzwehren Cem
05/12/18	Cousins, George Thomas	Pte	41754			kia	Fraize Churchyard
24/12/18	Radbourne, Henry John	Pte	13069		26	died	Riseberga Churchyard
29/12/18	Chamberlain, Oliver Charles	Pte	16127		26	died	Cologne Southern Cem

The enemy shell at Méricourt railway station 5th September 1918

Name	Rank	Number	Birthplace	Age	Cemetery Name
Britton, Clifford Kimberley	Pte	45837	Hanham		Dernancourt Comm Cem Ext
Bonham, Francis Edwin	Pte	45854	Wool	18	Méricourt-l'Abbé Comm Cem Ext
Carter, Cecil	Pte	45862	Hickeshall	18	Dernancourt Comm Cem Ext
Cartwright, Henry	Pte	45863	Wollescote		Méricourt-l'Abbé Comm Cem Ext
Cooper, Reginald Harry	Pte	45865	Headington	18	Méricourt-l'Abbé Comm Cem Ext
Clapham, Frederick	Pte	45868	Swindon	18	Dernancourt Comm Cem Ext
Coles, Arthur Bullen	Pte	45869	Bristol		Dernancourt Comm Cem Ext
Chapman, Clifford	Pte	45871	Radstock	18	Méricourt-l'Abbé Comm Cem Ext
Coburn, Frederick George	Pte	45872	Islington	18	Méricourt-l'Abbé Comm Cem Ext
Fowler, Sidney Robert	Pte	45889	Kingstanley	18	Méricourt-l'Abbé Comm Cem Ext
Hutchings, Reginald Edwin	Pte	45899	Plymouth	18	Dernancourt Comm Cem Ext
Hore, Henry Norman	Pte	45900	Bedford		Méricourt-l'Abbé Comm Cem Ext
Hughes, Benjamin	Pte	45903	Netherton		Méricourt-l'Abbé Comm Cem Ext
Jenkins, William Edward	Pte	45917	Shroton		Méricourt-l'Abbé Comm Cem Ext
Kingwell, William Richard	Pte	45922	Stonehouse	18	Dernancourt Comm Cem Ext
Loader, Stanley William	Pte	45923	Shepton Mallet	18	Méricourt-l'Abbé Comm Cem Ext
Lewis, Frederick Herbert	Pte	45924	Bristol	18	Méricourt-l'Abbé Comm Cem Ext
Passingham, Charles	Pte	45950	Malvern Link		Méricourt-l'Abbé Comm Cem Ext
Panter, Cyril Harley	Pte	45953		18	Méricourt-l'Abbé Comm Cem Ext
Painter, William	Pte	45955	South Cerney		Dernancourt Comm Cem Ext
Pratley, Reginald	Pte	45957	Dudley	20	Heilly Station Cemetery
Rowell, William Charles	Pte	45960	Paignton	18	Méricourt-l'Abbé Comm Cem Ext
Rogers, Henry Charles	Pte	45964	Southampton		Méricourt-l'Abbé Comm Cem Ext
Slade, Henry	Pte	45971	Portsmouth		Dernancourt Comm Cem Ext
Stone, Albert	Pte	45976	Exeter		Méricourt-l'Abbé Comm Cem Ext
Stokes, Victor	Pte	45981	Shaftesbury	18	Méricourt-l'Abbé Comm Cem Ext
Stone, Cecil Victor	Pte	45985	Newport	18	Méricourt-l'Abbé Comm Cem Ext
Smith, James Edward	Pte	45986	Portsmouth	18	Méricourt-l'Abbé Comm Cem Ext
Walden, John Martin	Pte	45992	Birmingham		Dernancourt Comm Cem Ext
Walden, William Richard	Pte	45998	Blockley		Méricourt-l'Abbé Comm Cem Ext

Appendix V

Appendix VI

Casualty statistics 1915 to 1918

Fatal casualties by rank by battalion

Rank	5th	6th	8th	Total
Lieutenant Colonel		1		1
Major	3		2	5
Captain	12	3	7	22
Lieutenant	8	5	10	23
2nd Lieutenant	33	26	27	86
RSM		1		1
Company Sgt Major	3	3	6	12
CQMS		1		1
Colour Sergeant	1			1
Sergeant	31	27	24	82
Lance Sergeant	10	8	11	29
Corporal	34	23	37	94
Lance Corporal	92	70	82	244
Private	819	495	771	2085
Total	1046	663	977	2686

A total of 2,686 men lost their lives while serving with the battalions. Although the 6th Battalion seems to have suffered less, it was disbanded in February 1918, so was on active service for 32 months, compared to 42 for the 5th Battalion and 40 for the 8th.

Fatal casualties by rank by year

Rank	1915	1916	1917	1918	Total
Lieutenant Colonel			1		1
Major	2		1	2	5
Captain	10	5	2	5	22
Lieutenant	9	3	5	6	23
2nd Lieutenant	10	37	21	18	86
RSM			1		1
Company Sgt Major	2	4	2	4	12
CQMS			1		1
Colour Sergeant			1		1
Sergeant	14	27	21	20	82
Lance Sergeant	4	16	4	5	29
Corporal	14	30	25	25	94
Lance Corporal	40	80	70	54	244
Private	339	601	530	615	2085
Totals	444	805	683	754	2686

The reduction of casualties among 2nd Lieutenants is noteworthy. The enthusiastic leaders of 1916, with distinctive uniforms and different weapons from their men paid heavily. By 1918, the experienced survivors had discarded badges of rank, and a more cautious approach to leadership succeeded in halving their casualty rate.

Fatal casualties by age by year

Of the 2,686 fatalities, 1,534 have their ages recorded by the CWGC, or the authors have obtained it from newspaper obituaries or other sources.

In 1916 and 1917, the majority of casualties were men in their twenties. By 1918, if the Royal Berks is typical, the BEF was much younger, and the greatest number of casualties occurred among young men who had been 14 or 15 when the war started.

Age at death	1915	1916	1917	1918	Total
17 to 19	51	53	35	162	301
20 to 24	97	155	138	130	520
25 to 29	56	127	70	82	335
30 to 34	30	50	77	50	207
35 to 39	17	44	45	28	134
40 to 44	6	10	8	4	28
45 to 49	2	4	2	0	8
50 +	0	1	0	0	1
Totals	259	444	375	456	1534

Buried or commemorated

Over half the fatalities, 51%, have no known grave, and their names are inscribed on the various memorials on the Western Front. 1,236 are buried in the Commonwealth War Graves Commission cemeteries in France or Belgium, 32 who died while prisoners of war are buried in Germany, and a further 60 in the United Kingdom.

Buried or commemorated in:	1915	1916	1917	1918	Total	P/cent
CWGC Cemetery, France or Belgium	121	367	272	476	1236	46%
CWGC Memorial, France or Belgium	309	412	396	241	1358	51%
CWGC Cemetery, Germany (POWs)	5	2	4	21	32	1%
UK Graveyard (Died of wounds at home)	9	24	11	16	60	2%
Total	444	805	683	754	2686	

Appendix VI

Age at death by rank

Gives the age at death by rank for the 1,534 men for whom we have their age

Age at death	Lt/Col, Majors	Capts & Lieuts	Warrant Officers	NCOs	Privates
17	-	-	-	-	10
18	-	1	-	5	81
19	-	6	-	21	177
20	-	6	-	16	92
21	-	13	-	24	77
22	-	10	-	21	70
23	-	7	-	23	69
24	-	9	-	19	64
25	-	7	-	22	53
26	-	7	-	14	61
27	-	6	1	12	42
28	-	3	-	9	39
29	1	7	1	13	37
30	-	4	-	11	35
31	-	3	-	8	38
32	-	-	1	4	31
33	-	5	1	5	22
34	1	2	1	7	28
35	-	1	1	8	26
36	-	3	-	6	22
37	-	-	2	2	28
38	1	-	-	4	17
39	1	-	-	3	9
40	1	3	-	2	6
41	-	-	-	-	3
42	-	-	-	1	6
43	-	2	-	-	1
44	-	-	-	-	3
45	-	-	-	-	3
46	-	-	-	-	2
47	-	-	-	2	-
49	-	-	-	-	1
53	-	-	-	1	-
Average Age	36	26	33	26	25

Attrition of the original battalions

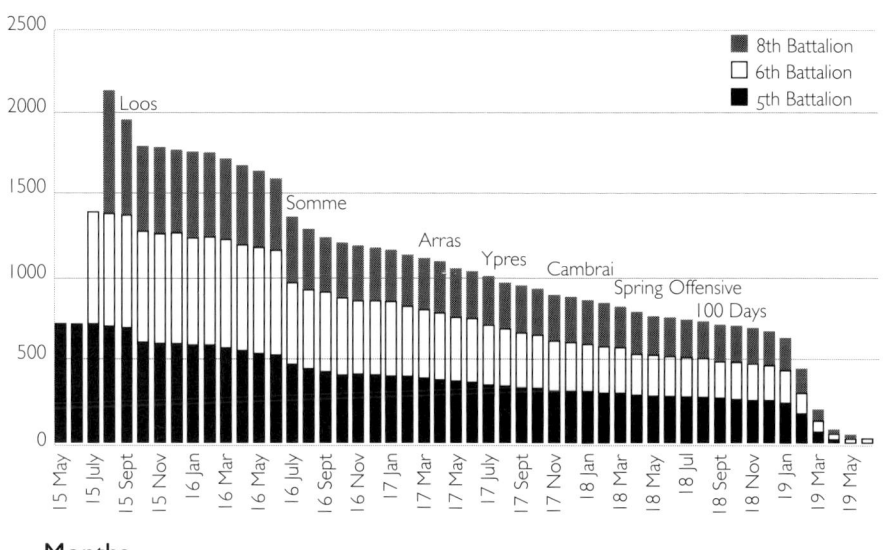

The three battalions went to France in May, July and August 1915, each with a nominal strength of 1,000 officers and men. They were thus entitled to wear the 1914/15 star, and the medal rolls for this decoration, held in the Public Record Office, give the date the recipient went to France, and his date and type of discharge. The vast majority of the types of discharge are: Killed, Discharged Medically Unfit, or, after the armistice, Demobilised, although a few were discharged as underage, or, in the case of regulars, expiry of service.

We have recorded the details of 2,165 men who went to France with the Royal Berkshire Regiment on the dates when the battalions are known to have travelled. We assume the 'missing' 800 either went on a different date, maybe with the transport sections, or perhaps were transferred to other units such as the Machine Gun Corps after arriving in France, and are included in the medal rolls under them.

The graph shows the attrition of the 2,165 as the war progressed. By November 1918, only 704 - less than a third - of the originals were still on active service, and very few of those were still with the battalion they started with. In February 1918, when the 6th Battalion was disbanded, and its men distributed to other Royal Berkshire battalions, only 102 of the original 752 remained.

The position is actually worse than is shown on the graph, as the men who were discharged as medically unfit through wounds would have spent some time in hospital and convalescence before assessment by a medical board and being formally discharged. We have used the date of discharge in the graph, but the man would have been wounded some time before this, when his active service effectively finished.

Appendix VI

Appendix VII

HONOURS AND AWARDS for the 5th, 6th and 8th Battalions of the Royal Berkshire Regiment as announced in the London Gazette in 1918/19 (The date of announcement is given in brackets)

5th Battalion

Distinguished Service Order
  Acting Lt Col **H T Goodland** (11.1.1919)
  Acting Lt Col **E H J Nicholls** M C
    (8.7.1918)
  Capt **John Milner Ready** M C (16.6.1918)

Military Cross
  2/Lt **William Herbert Ashby** (11.1.1919)
  2/Lt **Ian Robertson Baird** (26.7.1918)
  QM & Hon Capt **F F S Boshell**,
    (New Years Honours List 1918)
  Capt **Cyril Hands Cooke**
    (3.6.1916, King's Birthday Honours)
  2/Lt **Ernest William N Ellis** (1.2.1919)
  2/Lt **Charles Frederick Elsey**
    (3.6.1918 King's Birthday Honours)
  Acting Capt **J N Gregory** (16.9.1918)
  Acting Capt **B W Hougham** (1.2.1919)
  2/Lt **Reginald C Humphries** (1.2.1919)
  Lt **E G Joseph** (16.9.1918)
  Capt **C J Ludman** (8.3.1919 & 4.10.1919)
  Capt **Clifford Angus Mallam**
    (New Years Honours List 1918)
  Lt **Harold Kidd May**
    (18.2.1918 and 18.7.1918)
  2/Lt **Titus Philip Meyrick** (26.7.1918)
  Hon Lt and QM **J R Oxley** (16.8.1918)
  2/Lt **Frederick Charles Palmer** (1.2.1919)
  Acting Capt **Henry Arthur Rivers Pantlin**
    (New Years Honours List 1919)
  CSM 6859 **T A Perkins** (26.9.1916)
  2/Lt **Frank Powell** D C M, M M & Bar
    (2.4.1919 & 10.12.1919)
  2/Lt **J E Rickword**
    (8.3.1919 and 4.10.1919)
  2/Lt **William George Shilling** (1.2.1919)
  Lt **Alfred John Shipton** (26.7.1918)
  2/Lt **Eric Sparkes** (18.3.1919 & 4.10.1919)
  RSM 16689 **William Reginald Tilbury**
    (New Years Honours List 1919)
  Capt **J R West** (18.2.1918 & 18.7.1918)

Bar to Military Cross
  Capt **C A Mallam** M C (11.1.1919)
  Capt **J M Ready** D S O, M C (11.1.1919)

Distinguished Conduct Medal
  Acting Sgt 10058 **T H Davis** (3.10.1918)
  Acting Cpl 48674 **C E Gale** (3.10.1918)
  Pte 45671 **Ethelbert C Harvey** (16.1.1919)
  L/Cpl 14595 **R S Hayes** (3.10.1918)
  Sgt 16095 **P A V Leppard** (1.5.1918)
  Sgt 203031 (15665) **E Richmond** (3.9.1918)
  L/Sgt 24528 **J J Sargeant** M M (23.10.1918)
  Sgt 11268 **Charles Seymour** (1.5.1918)
  Sgt 10249 **William J Spokes** (3.9.1918)
  Sgt 16631 **Ernest Stokes** (2.3.1918)
  Sgt 24045 **F Varney** M M & Bar (3.9.1918)

Military Medal
  Cpl 39037 **J Armstrong** (11.2.1919)
  L/Cpl 23648 **A Bailey** (17.6.1919)

Pte 36235 **H T Baker** (7.10.1918)
Pte 10355 **Albert Bale** (19.3.1918)
Pte 9983 **G Barnes** (17.6.1919)
Pte 15316 **F Beech** (11.2.1919)
Pte 202913 **F Berry** (27.6.1918)
Cpl 48546 **E C Bickers** (7.10.1918)
Pte 10741 **Frederick Bland** (17.6.1919)
Cpl 17231 **S Breathwick** DCM (17.6.919)
Pte 48549 **P W Brimicombe** (23.7.1919)
Pte 43909 **A Brown** (7.10.1918)
Pte 19384 **A Budgen** (11.2.1919)
Pte 43945 **L Buffham** (23.7.1919)
Pte 27155 **John Bates Bushell** (13.9.1918)
Cpl 19444 **William H Butler** (16.7.1918)
Pte 39332 **John Carter** (7.10.1918)
Pte 17063 **Sidney H Clark** (7.10.1918)
Sgt 10224 **F C Coffey** (13.3.1918)
Sgt 7506 **Fred Cook** (11.2.1919)
L/Cpl 11123 **Albert C Cooper** (19.3.1918)
L/Cpl 28639 **C Cooper** (17.6.1919)
Sgt 220270 **R Cox** (11.2.1919)
Pte 10376 **Sidney Cripps** (11.2.1919)
Cpl 39312 **Edward Darkes** (23.7.1919)
Pte 45105 **W Drayton** (11.2.1919)
L/Cpl 10416 **C Edwards** (23.7.1919)
Sgt 12612 **W H Evans** (11.2.1919)
Sgt 12546 **T Felton** (11.2.1919)
Sgt 32153 **Harry France** (19.3.1918)
Pte 45111 **Albert Franklin** (17.6.1919)
Pte 27383 **J B Furber** (16.7.1918)
Pte 44826 **G Garrett** (17.6.1919)
Pte 43554 **W Gough** (23.7.1919)
Pte 10713 **G Grainger** (13.3.1918)
Pte 44327 **G Greaves** (11.6.1919)
L/Cp 45834 **Golby Gunthorpe** (17.6.1919)
L/Cpl 18497 **John F Gurr** (16.7.1918)
L/Cpl 10499 **F Hammon** (6.1.1918)
Pte 33769 **T W Hands** (11.2.1919)
Pte 48675 **H G Harper** (11.2.1919)
Cpl 10499 **F W Hermon** (19.3.1918)
Pte 48465 **L C Hermon**(Herman)(11.2.919)
Pte 200267 **George Hestor** (27.6.1918)

Sgt 23760 **E Heybourne** (February 1919)
Sgt 10461 **George Hillier** (17.4.1917)
Sgt 6087 **E Holmes** (11.2.1919)
Pte 200955 **C Hopgood** (7.10.1918)
Cpl **F J Howell** (13.3.1918)
CSM 12560 **E J Humphries** (23.7.1919)
Pte 10414 **Edward Irving** (23.7.1919)
Pte 48653 **J G Isham** (11.2.1919)
Pte 11714 **George Jackson** (12.6.1918)
Pte 160865 **Jones** (23.7.1919)
L/Cpl 11128 **W J Kent** (16.7.1918)
CSM 11251 **J B Lane** (23.7.1919)
L/Cpl 23718 **H C Littlefield** (16.7.1918)
Pte 11372 **W A Luckin** (17.6.1919)
Pte 43963 **A Martin** (20.10.1919)
L/Cpl 13039 **F May** (19.3.1918)
Pte 36127 **J W Mearns** (23.7.1919)
Pte 23604 **Arthur J Mizen** (11.2.1919)
Pte 18393 **John J H Money** (11.2.1919)
Pte 11001 **F P Munday** (17.6.1919)
Pte 202957 **P Nolan** (11.2.1919)
Pte 43914 **F J Osborne** (11.2.1919)
Pte 5615 **G Parkin** (11.2.1919)
Pte 11049 **W Payne** (23.7.1919)
Cpl 37361 **Thomas Pearce** (17.6.1919)
Sgt 41395 **C H Phillips** (23.7.1919)
Pte 11089 **Wallace Pickard** (23.7.1919)
Pte 203490 **A Plaskett** (11.2.1919)
Pte 11216 **W H Proctor** (17.6.1919)
L/Cpl 48580 **F G Puffet** (23.7.1919)
L/Cpl 9306 **Frederick Rudd** (19.3.1918)
Sgt 15559 **Percy Rumble** (20.10.1919)
Pte 11040 **A Sainsbury** (23.7.1919)
L/Cpl 48499 **E P Shipley** (23.7.1919)
Pte 220781 **Frederick Sinden** (11.2.1919)
Pte 44670 **F J L Smith** (17.6.1919)
Sgt 10042 **Ernest Albert Spicer** (7.10.1918)
Cpl 33343 **J Stanbridge** (17.6.1919)
Pte 35852 **E T Such** (14.1.1918)
Pte 22335 **Henry J Tanner** (11.2.1919)
Pte 7410 **G Turrell** (19.3.1918)
Pte 27075 **William Vasey** (17.6.1919)

L/Cpl **J Waddell** (17.6.1919)
Sgt 41401 **Charles H Warboys** (11.2.1919)
Sgt 10839 **W F Webster** (19.3.1918)
L/Cpl 11267 **H B Westfield** (23.7.1919)
Sgt 10796 **C F Whayling** (7.10.1918)
L/Cpl 43926 **R H Williams** (17.6.1919)
Cpl 38269 **A Wills** (11.2.1919)

Bar to Military Medal
Pte 10851 **T G Baker** M M (7.10.1918)
Sgt 10660 **G Bennett** M M (17.6.1919)
CSM **J H Bunce** M M (13.3.1919)
Sgt 10580 **F Burton** M M (12.3.1918)
L/Cpl 9376 **Albert Cox** M M (17.6.1919)
Pte 22278 **F J Coxhead** M M (23.7.1919)
L/Cpl 10563 **A Histead** M M (17.6.1919)
Cpl 12003 **R McAllister** M M (12.6.1918)
Cpl 18393 **J J H Money** M M (17.6.1919)
Sgt 24045 **F Varney** D C M, M M (16.7.1918)
Sgt 11793 **Herbert Watling** M M (14.5.1919)
Pte 15375 **John Worsfold** M M (17.6.1919)

2nd Bar to Military Medal
Sgt 9309 **G F Epsley** M M (19.3.1918)

Mentioned in Dispatches
Pte 39469 **P H Abell** (9.7.1919)
L/Cpl 10651 **A Barnes** (9.7.1919)
Pte 11167 **Charles Brennand** (28.12.1918)
Capt **G E Collins** (9.7.1919)
Major **T V B Dennis** (24.5.1918)
Lt **C F Elsey** (28.12.1918)
Acting Lt Col **H T T Goodland** D S O (28.12.1918)
Cpl 16959 **R E Humphries** (28.12.1918)
Cpl 11037 **F Loader** (9.7.1919)
QMS 3/10224 **J W Montague** (24.5.1918)

Meritorious Service Medal
Sgt 9018 **Ivern Deacon** (17.6.1918)
CQMS **W Girling** (3.6.1919)
Sgt 17019 **A T Griffiths** (3.6.1919)

Pte **Herbert Wiliam Peacock** (17.6.1918)
CSM 73285 **Pibworth** (3.6.1919)
RQMS 8215 **Charles Pike** (18.1.1919)
Sgt 10519 **G Randall** (3.6.1919)
Sgt 16440 **Albert E Trinder** (18.1.1919)

Foreign Decoration
Croix de Guerre (Belgian)
Lt **Malcolm Bartlett Beattie** (11.3.1918)
Pte 19012 **Phillip Langman** (12.7.1918)

6th Battalion

Distinguished Service Order
Capt **R Adair Rochfort** M C (18.1.1918)

Military Cross
Lt **Arthur Alan Barrett** (26.7.1918)
2/Lt **W T Lord** M M (June 1918)
2/Lt **H A Mossman** (18.1.1918)
Lt **J W K Wernham** (18.1.1918 & 25.4.1918)

Distinguished Conduct Medal
Sgt 37352 **Alfred Richard Albury** (3.9.1918)
Pte 12400 **C W Ashley** (4.3.1918)
Cpl 6259 **Arthur F Chivers** (4.3.1918)
Pte 36329 **Harry Gates** (4.3.1918)
Pte 36565 **Charles W Graves** (4.3.1918)
Cpl 24528 **J J Sargeant** M M (3.10.1918)
Sgt 10123 **Walter George Trinder** (1.1.1918)
L/Cpl 36969 **W Walker** (28.3.1918)

Military Medal
L/Cpl 15507 **Henry Alderman** (23.2.1918)
Cpl 7454 **H G Bartlett** (16.7.1918)
L/Cpl 12539 **John H Callcott** (23.2.1918)
Pte 18743 **Arthur Cox** (13.3.1918)
Pte 37231 **R J Dean** (23.2.1918)
Pte 12037 **T A Fletcher** (23.2.1918)
Sgt **W A Gillingham** (16.7.1918)
Pte 36903 **Walter Godfrey** (13.3.1918)
Pte **J H Grout** (16.7.1918)

Sgt 8209 **Thomas G Huggins** (13.3.1918)
Sgt 17560 **G Lawson** (23.2.1918)
Sgt 12056 **A Millgrove** D C M (23.2.1918)
Pte 22131 **Frank Morgan** (23.2.1918)
Pte 11995 **W J Patrick** (16.7.1918)
Pte 202981 **Joseph Smith** (23.2.1918)
L/Cpl 12700 **E Sterry** (23.2.1918)
Pte 36498 **Stuart T Williams** (23.2.1918)

Bar to Military Medal
Sgt 3016 (200795) **John William Lambourne** M M (14.1.1918)
Pte 200767 **Rowland G Ludlow** M M (28.1.1918)

Mentioned in Dispatches
Acting CQMS 12987 **H J Bevan** (24.5.1918)
Actg CQMS 16561 **W J Kimpton** (9.7.1919)
Cpl 12591 **G Parker** (24.5.1918)
Capt **V R Price** (24.5.1918)
CQMS 10180 **A Tidmarsh** (24.5.1918)

Meritorious Service Medal
RQMS 10367 **C H Robertson** (17.6.1918)

Foreign Decorations
Croix de Guerre (Belgian)
Pte 19012 **P Langman** (12.7.1918)
Pte 12675 **A T Preece** (12.7.1918)

8th Battalion

Distinguished Service Order
Lt Col **T N Banks** M C (15.10.1918)
Lt Col **N B Hudson** M C (8.3.1919)

Bar to Distinguished Service Order
Lt Col **N B Hudson** D S O, M C (8.3.1919)

Military Cross
2/Lt **William Angel** M M (1.2.1919)
2/Lt **Walter Frederick Bizley** (26.7.1918)
2/Lt. **N H G Blackburn** (1.2.1919)

Lt **C F R Bland** (18.1.1918 & 25.4.1918)
Lt **Aubrey Mellish Bray** (16.9.1918)
Acting Major **W H Ferguson** M D, RAMC (16.9.1918)
2/Lt **James Grant** (1.2.1919)
2/Lt **T C Halliburton** (1.2.1919)
2/Lt **Percival Charles Leggeter** (8.3.1919)
2/Lt **D N Lewin** (2.4.1919 & 10.12.1919)
2/Lt **Harry Martin** (1.2.1919)
Lt **Frewen Moor** (18.1.1918 & 25.4.1918)
Capt **G W H Nicholson** (1.2.1919)
2/Lt **G F Parrott** (2.4.1919 & 10.12.1919)
Capt **Frederick David Phillips** (3.6.1918, King's Birthday Honours List)
2/Lt **Frank Joseph Powell** D C M, M M (2.4.1919 & 10.12.1919)
Lt **C E B Rogers** (23.4.1918)
Lt **Hugh Le Gallienne Sarchet** (1.1.1918, New Years Honours List)
2/Lt **Fred Spearey** (1.2.1919)
Major **Stephen Winter Warr** (1.2.1919)

Bar to Military Cross
Capt **P B Bellanger** M C, M D, RAMC (26.7.1918)
Capt **W H Ferguson** M C, M D, RAMC (8.3.1918 & 4.10.1919)
Capt **G W H Nicholson** M C (1.2.1919)
Lt **T K Pickard** M C (1.2.1919)
Capt **J N Richardson** M C (16.9.1918)
Capt **N Wykes** M C (1.2.1919)

Distinguished Conduct Medal
Sgt 38698 5 **Bagnall** (16.1.1919)
Pte 37096 **W Griffiths** (16.1.1919)
Acting Sgt 16106 **J J Hurst** (16.1.1919)
L/Sgt 200631 **G W Hutchins** (16.1.1919)
Cpl 10198 **J C Masters** (12.3.1919)
Pte 17256 **R Mellish** (3.6.1918)
Pte 36687 **Joseph Edward Peters** (3.9.1918)
Pte 45958 **J A Preston** (18.2.1919)
Sgt 14571 **H S Smith** (1.1.1919)

Sgt 10249 **William John Spokes** (3.9.1918)
CSM 27221 **Richard Webb** (28.3.1918)

Military Medal

L/Cpl 36222 **Percy H Abbott** (13.3.1919)
L/Cpl 18079 **Ernest P Ayres** (23.2.1918)
Cpl 44535 **Cyril C Bemrose** 913.3.1919)
Pte 44682 **Albert T Benneton** (13.3.1919)
Pte 44767 **Thomas Blakey** (13.3.1919)
Pte 18571 **Harry Butcher** (23.2.1918)
Pte 13261 **A J Butler** (14.5.1919)
Pte 20148 **Benjamin Butler** (23.2.1919)
Pte 43720 **Eric Butler** (13.3.1919)
Pte 39326 **H S Butler** (31.12.1918)
Cpl 10451 **Samuel J Caller** (17.6.1919)
Pte 14108 **L D Chapman** (29.8.1918)
Cpl 41605 **W Clements** (23.7.1919)
Sgt 10224 **Frederick C Coffey** (13.3.1918)
Pte 44992 **T H Coffield** (23.7.1919)
Cpl 207746 **Harry Compton** (17.6.1919)
Sgt 220755 **John L Cowie** (23.7.1919)
Pte 44594 **A F Crutch** (24.1.1919)
Pte 39326 **H L Cutler** (23.7.1919)
L/Cpl 45637 **George Dean** (17.6.1919)
L/Cpl 201168 **George A Dell** (13.3.1919)
Cpl 45612 **R Douglas** (23.7.1919)
L/Cpl 21825 **J C Enoch** (23.2.1918)
Pte 23691 **W Excell** (17.6.1919)
Pte 37660 **A F Filmore** (24.1.1919)
Sgt 20043 **E Goodchild** (24.1.1919)
Cpl 14343 **G W Gunner** (24.1.1919)
Pte 35013 **C F Hackwood** (13.3.1919)
Sgt 200130 **F G Hale** (13.3.1919)
Pte 39386 **E C Harris** (13.3.1919)
Pte 11205 **F S Hawkes** (13.3.1919)
Pte 45912 **C F Hodges** (23.7.1919)
Cpl 200459 **P G Holloway** (13.3.1919)
Pte 21863 5 **Hopes** (29.8.1918)
Pte 43789 **H Inscoe** (23.7.1919)
Pte 18159 **A E James** (13.3.1919)
Pte 45064 5 **G Jerrom** (23.7.1919)
L/Cpl 184354 **F G Kane** (13.3.1919)

Pte 45068 **V E Light** (23.7.1919)
Sgt 202406 **W W Longman** (13.3.1919)
L/Cpl 220739 **J Lovell** (23.7.1919)
Sgt 45640 **H Lunnon** (13.3.1919)
Pte 14099 **G T Luxford** (13.3.1919)
Pte 44725 **N Nallin** (24.1.1919)
Cpl 28728 **J J Marshall** (23.7.1919)
Pte 14891 **C Nillington** (23.2.1918)
Pte 14323 **G H Morgan** (23.2.1918)
L/Cpl 13099 **E H Noyes** (29.8.1918)
Pte 43674 **H Pitchfork** (23.7.1919)
Pte 132144(200893) **E J Pocock** (20.10.1919)
Pte 27589 **H Pottinger** (13.3.1919)
L/Cpl 37895 **A J Rawlings** (17.6.1919)
Sgt 9691 **W Ross** (13.3.1919)
Pte 31592 **H J Rowdiffe** (23.7.1919)
CSM, Acting RSM 44990 **J E Saunders**
    (13.3.1919)
Pte 13180 **W J Shears** (13.3.1919)
Pte 220162 **F Skelton** (23.7.1919)
Cpl, Actg Sgt **W Slatterthwaite** (13.3.1919)
Sgt 13093 **A R Smith** (23.2.1918)
L/Sgt 44070 **Christopher Smith** (13.3.1919)
Cpl 11690 **F G Smith** (24.1.1919)
Pte 43706 **G Smith** (13.3.1919)
Pte 18268 **George Sparrow** (23.7.1919)
Pte 44644 **L F Sparrow** (23.7.1919)
Pte 202497 **H Stearns** (24.1.1919)
Pte 14654 **F W Stephens** 29.8.1918)
Pte 44747 **E R Stone** (13.3.1919)
Pte 12949 **W J Street** (23.7.1919)
Pte 37374 **A Strong** (13.3.1919)
L/Cpl 9123 **A W Underwood** (13.3.1919)
Pte 36869 **A J White** (6.8.1918)
Sgt 84331 **J E White** (23.7.1919)
Pte 18480 **J W White** (23.7.1919)
Cpl 17936 **E F Wiles** (23.2.1918)
Pte 10192 **H Wilmott** (13.3.1919)

Bar to Military Medal

Pte 19013 **Fred Bailey** M M (29.8.1918)
Pte 14494 **John Donovan** M M (23.2.1918)

Sgt 9789 **G T Funnel** M M (11.2.1919)
Sgt 12887 **E Gray** M M (13.3.1919)
Sgt 19002 **E J Joy** M M (23.2.1918)
Sgt 200633 **R E Lambden** M M (13.3.1919)
Cpl 203843 **J Nazey** M M (1919)

Mentioned in Dispatches
Pte 13106 **C Dyer** (28.12.1918)
Pte 33323 **F Dyer** (9.7.1919)
Acting Sgt 13648 **W H Goodey** (9.7.1919)
Lt Col **N B Hudson** D S O, M C (9.7.1919)
Sgt 121045 **Long** (9.7.1919)
QM & Temp Lt 121045 **C Noon**
   (December 1918)
2/Lt **E Wallis** (24.5.1918)
Capt **G J H Walls** (28.12.1918)
L/Cpl 15564 **J W Woodrow** (28.12.1918)
Capt **N Wykes** M C (9.7.1919)

Meritorious Service Medal
Sgt 36728 **John H Cox** (3.6.1919)
CQMS 10503 **Harry Dodd** (17.6.1918)
Sgt 14860 **F C Hinton** (18.1.1919)
Pte 11541 **A Syer** (3.6.1919)
Sgt 14261 **T Thomas** (1.1.1918)
Actg L/Sgt 15564 **W J Woodrow** (3.6.1919)

Foreign Decorations
Croix de Guerre (Belgian)
Capt **David John Footman** (13.7.1918)
Pte 9688 **William Alfred Mason**
   (12.7.1918)
Cpl 18480 **James William White**
   (12.7.1918)

N.B. The London Gazette indicates only the regiments, not the battalions, in which the men were serving when the honour or award was approved. Some of the above who served in more than one battalion of the Royal Berkshire Regiment may have been serving in a different battalion at the time of the award. Others may have been omitted.

Sources published

Official publications

War Office, *Officers Died in the Great War 1914–19* (n.e. Polstead: 1988)

War Office, *Soldiers Died in the Great War 1914–19* Pt. 52 (n.e. Polstead: 1989)

Edmonds, J.E., *Military Operations France & Belgium, 1918* Vol.1 (London: 1935)
Vol. 2 (London: 1937)
Vol. 4 (London: 1947)
Vol. 5 (London: 1948)

Newspapers and journals

Berkshire Chronicle
Maidenhead Advertiser
Newbury Weekly News
Reading Mercury
Reading Standard
Berkshire and the War: The Reading Standard Pictorial Record, (Reading: 1916–19)
China Dragon: The Journal of the Royal Berkshire Regiment, (Princess Charlotte of Wales's), 1914–59
The Journal of the Duke of Edinburgh's Royal Regiment, (Berkshire and Wiltshire), 1959–94

Other works

Bourne, J.M., *Britain and the Great War 1914–18* (London: 1989)

Falls, C., *The First World War,* (London: 1960)

French, D., *The Strategy of the Lloyd George Coalition 1916–18* (Oxford: 1995)

Middlebrook, M., *The Kaiser's Battle* (London: 1978)

Montgomery, Maj-Gen Sir A., *The Story of the Fourth Army in the Battles of the Hundred Days* (London: 1919)

Nichols, G.H.F., *The 18th Division in the Great War* (London 1922)

Petre, F. Loraine, *The Royal Berkshire Regiment* (Reading: 1925)

Prior, R. & Wilson, T., *Command on the Western Front* (Oxford: 1992)

Scott, A.B. & Brumwell, P.M., *History of the 12th (Eastern) Division in the Great War* (London: 1923)

Simpson, A., *The Evolution of Victory* (London: 1995)

Terraine, J., *To Win a War. 1918 The Year of Victory* (London: 1978)

Wilson, T., *The Myriad Faces of War* (Cambridge: 1986)

Sources unpublished

Public Record Office, Kew

War Diaries (WO 95)

94	Tank Corps
110	4th Tank Battalion
678	III Corps
681	III Corps
1826	12th Division
1827	12th Division
1855	36th Brigade
1856	5th Battalion, Royal Berkshire Regiment
2017	18th Division
2036	53rd Brigade
2037	6th & 8th Battalions, Royal Berkshire Regiment

Officers records (WO 339)

26109	Captain D Footman
60807	Lieutenant N Langston
58882	Lieutenant E J Mecey
3313	Lieutenant F M Sumpster

Imperial War Museum, London

Papers of H Harding, 5th Battalion, Royal Berkshire Regiment

Papers of A J Gosling, 6th Battalion, Royal Berkshire Regiment

The Royal Gloucestershire, Berkshire and Wiltshire Regiment (Salisbury) Museum

War Diaries

5th, 6th and 8th Battalions, Royal Berkshire Regiment

Papers of J W Randall, 8th Battalion, Royal Berkshire Regiment

In private hands

Papers of S W Tarrant, 5th Battalion, Royal Berkshire Regiment
(Mrs M Gyngell)

VICTORY

Wishing You The BEST OF LUCK AND A HAPPY XMAS

·1919· BLIGHTY
·1918· MALARD WOOD / LA BOISSELLE / TRONES WOOD
·1917· PASSCHENDAELE
·1916· CONTALMAISON / HIGH WOOD / BAZENTIN
·1915· LOOS
·1914· BLIGHTY.

8th Battⁿ ROYAL BERKSHIRE REGT.

Ernest
"Beauvoir"